"What a veritable garden of delights this collection of essays is! Organic, knowledgeable and insightful. Pirbhai recounts her journey as an 'émigré-settler' in a fine poetic style, tripping down memory lane with ease, building a rich tapestry of deliciously vivid memories stretching across continents. Her political awareness and cultural depth are layered with humour and self-irony. I was genuinely sorry when I got to the end." – Rukhsana Ahmad, author of *Song for a Sanctuary* and *River on Fire*

"A novice tree planter and gardener and self-described émigré-settler on Indigenous lands in Canada, Mariam Pirbhai's cascading essays in *Garden Inventories: Reflections on Land, Place and Belonging* are an enticing *metaphoray*, as Robin Wall Kimmerer states it, a walk through one's world with all of the senses – mind, body, emotion, spirit and imagination – in search of home. Pirbhai's keen observations of North American obsessions in gardening, her musings aloud on land and ownership, and the often unspoken relationship with Indigenous peoples, are informative and revealing. She invites readers to take a meditative walk through time with her as she names, compares, evaluates and reconciles the life of plants and trees native and non-native to North America, to the Grand River region and to the small garden that she and her husband tend to in southern Ontario." – Rita Bouvier, author of *A Beautiful Rebellion* and *nakamowin' sa for the seasons*

"At a time of increasing dislocation around the globe and a massive re-evaluation of what it means to have the pleasure and privilege of roots in a place, Mariam Pirbhai's *Garden Inventories: Reflections on Land, Place and Belonging* asks us whether there are other ways to create and sustain relationships with the land besides birthright. Moving from the many locations she has called home over the years to the small piece of land on which she currently lives and gardens with her husband, Pirbhai notes, 'We have brought our own stories of land and homeland to this garden, as we listen carefully to the stories that it has, in turn, shared with us.' Whether exploring on the keen focus on gardening in North America or the fraught concept of land 'ownership,' she is, above all things, attending closely to place and holding her many landscapes in intimate, revealing conversation." – Jenna Butler, author of *Revery: A Year of Bees* and *A Profession of Hope: Farming on the Edge of the Grizzly Trail*

"*Garden Inventories* explores ways to decolonize our desire to create home on native land. Mariam Pirbhai and her husband are descendants of immigrants from Pakistan and Guatemala. For the last seventeen years, they've been making home in Waterloo, Ontario. Their migrant histories have given them contrapuntal vision that sees between what they learned in other places and the place where they now live. It's not lost on them that their new neighbourhood is called Colonial Acres. In essays that defamiliarize the global migration of roses, the cultural hegemony of lawns, the multigenerational rite of 'going to the cottage' and their effects on Indigenous lives and biomes, Pirbhai tracks between what she learned from the *lands that were* and what she's now learning from the *land that is* about how to participate in a new balance that can foster a healthy *land that will be* for the future." – Daniel Coleman, author of *Yardwork: A Biography of an Urban Place*

Garden Inventories

[signature]
(Nov. '23)

Also by Mariam Pirbhai

Fiction
Isolated Incident
Outside People and Other Stories

Nonfiction
Critical Perspectives on Indo-Caribbean Women's Literature (co-editor)
Mythologies of Migration, Vocabularies of Indenture: Novels of the South Asian Diaspora in Africa, the Caribbean, and Asia-Pacific

Garden Inventories

Reflections on Land, Place and Belonging

Mariam Pirbhai

WOLSAK
& WYNN

© Mariam Pirbhai, 2023

All images courtesy of the author.

No part of this publication may be reproduced, stored in a retrieval system or transmitted, in any form or by any means, without the prior written consent of the publisher or a license from the Canadian Copyright Licensing Agency (Access Copyright). For an Access Copyright license, visit www.accesscopyright.ca or call toll free to 1-800-893-5777.

Published by Wolsak and Wynn Publishers
280 James Street North
Hamilton, ON L8R2L3
www.wolsakandwynn.ca

Editor: Noelle Allen | Copy editor: Ashley Hisson
Cover and interior design: Jen Rawlinson
Cover image: Mariam Pirbhai
Author photograph: Ronaldo Garcia
Typeset in Adobe Caslon Pro and Larken
Printed by Brant Service Press Ltd., Brantford, Canada

Printed on certified 100% post-consumer Rolland Enviro Paper.

10 9 8 7 6 5 4 3 2 1

  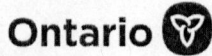

 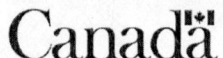

The publisher gratefully acknowledges the support of the Canada Council for the Arts and the Ontario Arts Council. We also acknowledge the financial support of the Government of Canada through the Canada Book Fund and the Government of Ontario through the Ontario Book Publishing Tax Credit and Ontario Creates.

Library and Archives Canada Cataloguing in Publication

Title: Garden inventories : reflections on land, place and belonging / Mariam Pirbhai.
Names: Pirbhai, Mariam, 1970- author.
Description: Includes bibliographical references.
Identifiers: Canadiana 20230502350 | ISBN 9781989496770 (softcover)
Subjects: LCGFT: Essays.
Classification: LCC PS8631.I73 G37 2023 | DDC C814/.6—dc23

To Ronaldo,
and Our Neighbours

Contents

The Land That Is   /1

Contrapuntal Gardeners   /19

By Any Other Name   /39

Anthropology of the Cottage,
or a (Second?) Slice of Precambrian Pie   /63

Garden Inventories   /93

Startling Lawn Facts   /127

Not Your Garden-Variety Settlement Story   /153

Acknowledgements   /157

Notes   /159

The Land That Is

How long has it taken me to see, to really begin to see, this land? How long to stop looking over my shoulder, in the sometimes-bitter-sometimes-mournful-sometimes-yearning-sometimes-snivelling window of nostalgia? As I gaze outside my window at the little clump of lanky Jack pine trees we inherited on this property in the city of Waterloo, in southwestern Ontario, and the white pines we've planted as the Jack pines dwindle in number, I know that I have only begun to see the *land that is* on a timetable that is uniquely mine. Seventeen years.

Seventeen years and counting. Seventeen is such an unremarkable number. An odd number in a society that often celebrates evens. Numerologists might disagree: 1+7=8. Eight signifies balance, harmony. Seventeen years ago, my husband, Ronaldo Garcia, and I moved from Montreal, Quebec, to Waterloo, Ontario. Seventeen years ago, we bought and settled in our current home, where we recently celebrated twenty-five years of togetherness. (And who would deny *twenty-five* its numerical clout.)

Seventeen was also the age at which both Ronaldo and I immigrated to Canada as our parents' dependents – his family arriving from Guatemala and mine, via a rather circuitous route, from Pakistan. One might even say that seventeen years, for Ronaldo and I, has twenty-five-year currency – that is, it's a veritable milestone for two people who had never before lived in any one house for more than three or four years apiece. In fact, the *first* seventeen years of my life were lived across three continents (Asia, Europe and North America), five countries (Pakistan, England, the United Arab Emirates, the Philippines and Canada), seven cities and, yes, *seventeen* different dwellings.

Is this, our house in the suburbs, complete with land ownership and title deeds, the sum total of every migrant's dream? Is this material stake in the land our passport to belonging? And yet, the

The Land That Is

questions persist: Are we rooted here? If all acts of naturalization are made equal, how do we know that we are rooted? How long does it take to feel rooted, anyway? That old catalpa tree across the street, its arms now reaching out to kiss a Norway maple on the other side, might say fifty years or more. The first generation might say it takes the next generation to feel truly rooted. Is rootedness, then, enjoyed exclusively by virtue of birthright – that is, being born in a place, where things like family, genealogy, heritage and home are as securely anchored as glacial sediment veining Precambrian rock? Or can we arrive at such states by other channels and means?

Over the last seventeen years, Ronaldo and I have tended this little square pocket of land that is our garden in the northernmost edge of the Carolinian life zone, a semi-temperate climatic region hugging Ontario's southwestern border. We have brought our own stories of land and homeland to this garden, as we listen carefully to the stories it has, in turn, shared with us. We live in a region known for holding the warmest average annual temperatures and highest levels of biodiversity in Canada, but where much of this natural abundance has been lost to colonization, agriculture and urbanization, in what is also the most densely populated cradle of the nation.[1] We live in one of the richest forested terrains, where black walnuts and oaks were guided to regenerate themselves by acts of Indigenous fire stewardship, such as "cultural burning" practiced by the Anishinaabeg or, in this stretch of Ontario, by the Mississauga peoples.[2] And yet, when I walk through conservation sites, it is the black walnut and oak that stand neglected or at risk, their fruits left unharvested and uneaten by all but the squirrels and birds who continue the work of replenishment.

Our tiny pocket of land sits in a province that could fit two

Garden Inventories

Germanies or four United Kingdoms into its one-million-square-kilometre pocket. This is a land of staggering distances sandwiched between four great lakes – Erie, Huron, Ontario and Superior – and, somewhere far, far off, in a northerly direction, the polar Arctic currents of James Bay, but also a land where one can feel decidedly landlocked. Where SUVs and NAFTA-sanctioned trucks duke it out for supremacy on some of the world's busiest highways, but it's still possible to have a chance encounter with a coyote or white-tailed deer on a walk through the woods and, for some, even to the corner store. Where melting ice and rainfall trickle into storm drains that empty out into streams and creeks running alongside cookie-cutter housing developments built far too close to rivers and lakes. Where neighbourhoods like ours are nestled in a place that has come to be known as the Grand River region, whose watershed is approximately the size of Prince Edward Island, Canada's smallest, but by no means small, Atlantic province. Where the Grand River travels some three hundred kilometres, from the Dufferin County highlands just south of Georgian Bay to Lake Erie, the eleventh largest freshwater lake in the world.

The Grand River region is a pocket of land within this great land where the number six assumed historical significance when Britain obtained permission from the Mississaugas, recognized in the eighteenth century as the "Aboriginal occupants" of this region, to grant safe haven to their Indigenous allies during the American (Revolutionary) War of Independence.[3] These allies were the Haudenosaunee Peoples unified under the Six Nations Confederacy, made up of the Mohawk, Onondaga, Oneida, Seneca, Cayuga and the Tuscarora peoples. The Mississaugas granted the Confederacy the use of six miles running on each side of the Grand River, from source to mouth, an agreement between First

The Land That Is

Peoples ratified by British imperial seals in the Haldimand Treaty of 1784.[4] This, too, is the land we call home – a place where royal proclamations such as the Haldimand Treaty, which came to shape this land's colonial contours, are all too often buried and obfuscated by the claiming and reclaiming, naming and renaming, mapping and remapping of the land.

This book is not a migrant's memoir of continental crossings so much as an émigré-settler's sketchbook of the immediate world outside her front door. It cares not for departures so much as arrivals. Like arriving at a place of acceptance that this world outside my front door will always be informed by my sensibility as an émigré – that is, as someone with other lands and places in my mind's eye. In my case, with a plurality of lands and places, like a geographic kaleidoscope. As such, a book about this land – *the land that is* – will invariably be overlaid with traces of *the lands that were* – those other places to which I have also belonged.

Coming as I do from a once colonized land – the Indian subcontinent, the oldest and longest held territory of the British Empire – it is impossible not to see *the land that is*, ravaged and plundered as it has been, through the historical ripples and echoes of colonialism meted out to other peoples in faraway lands. I am born to parents and grandparents who crossed the historic threshold from India to Pakistan because a hastily drawn border known as the Radcliffe Line (drawn up by a British lawyer who had never before set foot on the Indian subcontinent) told them they were no longer home, no longer welcome on one or the other side of this newly partitioned land. In 1947, Partition displaced fourteen million people in a mass exodus across this blood-soaked line;

for many South Asian Canadian families now multiply displaced from their ancestral homes in the Indian subcontinent, Partition still registers as a familial and historical legacy carried across other borders on journeys to other lands.[5]

These stories of Empire, anti-imperial revolution and decolonization have necessarily followed me into a neighbourhood unselfconsciously called Colonial Acres, and I can't help but wonder how these historical echoes inform or even shape my relationship to this land. Can émigrés afford to carry such historical baggage across the threshold of yet another land? Conversely, can émigrés ignore their own position as another kind of occupant — dare I say, a new kind of settler — on Indigenous lands? What might it take to cultivate a different relationship to this land, or even to this small part of the land known as the Grand River region? This place where winter sets in long before its official arrival on December 21, and remains stubbornly in place several months after its official conclusion on March 21. This land where the growing season is shorter than an academic term, and sinking one's hands into the soil before it freezes again is a fleeting pleasure, a perennial gift to be savoured. This land where more often than not we find ourselves battling against the loss of land — green spaces and conservation areas, creeks and river trails — all those protected areas that give us a sense of connection and belonging to something beyond the foundations and fences we erect and maintain. This land where semi-temperate forests lie on the brink of extinction or extirpation; where townships are also places at risk of losing their social and ecological identity as they fast develop into another metropolis, another outlying branch of the GTA (Greater Toronto Area); where the ever-diminishing forest is a constant reminder of cultures and heritages at risk, and where an émigré-settler might also feel like an entity at risk — at risk of losing a part of her own equatorial sensibility in this northern environment.

The Land That Is

Ronaldo and I met while I was a graduate student in Montreal and he, a college professor in Joliette, Quebec. Ours was a classic encounter of the Canadian kind, where two émigrés, or the children of émigrés, from parts of the world that are little known one to another, randomly meet and share stories about these distant places, and how or why they left them. They are overcome by how easy, how natural, how cathartic it is to share these stories with each other, especially because they are the kind of stories not everyone cares to hear. They are quick to see that the factors that spit them out of their respective countries of birth are similar only insofar as they were precipitated by political forces disrupting any hope of peace for their families, a saga on instant replay in the destiny of most postcolonial nations. A story so commonplace by now that it hardly bears repeating: simply substitute one colonizer for another (Britain, Spain, France, et cetera); replace one puppet regime with another (if by chance a democratically elected government comes along, anticipate a bloody coup largely operated by foreign interests championing democracy, which will rob the people who elected said government of their democracy); throw neocolonial operatives, multinational corporations, local despots, military regimes and profiteering mercenaries into the mix; and stir, stir, stir. The outcome is always the same: fight or flight for the people. Ronaldo's parents chose flight. My parents chose flight. Ronaldo's parents took a one-way ticket to Montreal, Quebec. My parents flittered and fluttered from one city to another, one continent to another, before landing in Halifax, Nova Scotia.

You might say that Ronaldo and I found "home" in each other's company, recognizing something of that migrant's plight. But, as it turned out, we have both spent much of our lives in Canada (be it with our families, as independents, or as a couple) in various states of transience. We packed a lot of boxes, returned the keys to numerous homes, because life just kept us moving, as it tends to do. Financial exigencies, parents' separations, academic paths, professional opportunities . . . life doesn't come to a standstill just because you've got a newly minted passport that confirms your arrival as a "naturalized" citizen, as if a piece of paper, albeit a highly valuable and coveted one, confers upon you an innate sense of rootedness, of belonging. Even roots are in constant motion, below ground.

Eventually, Ronaldo and I moved out of a condo and bought our first property with a tiny piece of land in a place called Ville Saint-Laurent, an outlying borough of Montreal. This was shortly after I completed a Ph.D. in English literature, and Ronaldo had published the first of several books on computer languages like Linux and Red Hat that I still can't speak. It was finally time to catch our breath. To feel the ground beneath our feet. But we barely had time to unpack much less tend our new little patch of lawn before one of those professional opportunities knocked on my door in the form of a tenure-track position at Wilfrid Laurier University, in Waterloo, Ontario. Seeing that tenure-track jobs in narrowly specialized fields were as hard to come by as a winning lotto ticket, especially for someone who checked several minority boxes (person of colour, very long-haired female in a short-haired male-dominated profession), and seeing as Waterloo was also known as the "Silicon Valley" of Canada, where Ronaldo could foresee a career change after twenty-five years in teaching, we honoured the tradition our parents had so ably established for us. We packed up another home with maximum efficiency and minimal fuss, and moved again.

Montreal had also become a haunted place because my mother, Qamar Pirbhai (née Iqbal), had recently passed at the age of sixty. I was shattered by the loss. Everywhere I went – east, south, north,

The Land That Is

west – the last anguish-filled weeks of my mother's life choked me with grief. Montreal, the city I had fallen in love with for its artistry and conviction of identity, had stomped on my heart and I could no longer look at it through a lover's eyes. Both my mother and Ronaldo's father, Catalino Garcia, now lay buried, side by side, under a cherry tree in a multifaith cemetery, and it seemed as good a time as any to make a fresh start. For Ronaldo, leaving Montreal wasn't as clear-cut as all that – he was the caregiver to his aging mother, Rebeca Gonzalez. Quebec had been home to his family since the 1970s, when they were among the first wave of Latin Americans to settle in the province. Ronaldo would also be retiring French, the second language he had lived and worked in for over thirty years and, in my case, the third language I had struggled to live and work in for a decade. Montreal wasn't home in the white-picket-fence sort of way, but it was his home in a way that it was never mine.

Moving to anglophone Ontario, the massive province that most immigrants – at least South Asian immigrants – gravitate toward like moths to the strobe lights of the CN Tower, was not without its challenges. But interprovincial migrations seemed like a cinch after our transcontinental crossings. And since this last big move from Montreal to Waterloo, we have managed to set a new precedent for ourselves: we have lived in this one home for seventeen consecutive years. Seventeen years of relative stillness. To the multiply displaced, achieving such stillness over time is nothing short of revelation. It affords a level of constancy and consistency – as homeowners, as neighbours and, in our case, as "naturalized" citizens – that starts to become a new way of seeing, of looking, of being in the world.

Garden Inventories

This one home in this one city has begun to yield some gifts of sight. I have seen my immediate environment, this neighbourhood called Colonial Acres, transformed in ways that only locals can, like the year culverts were brought to our street, destroying, as some residents argued, its country-like setting (namely, one without streetlights or pavements); or that time one of the friendliest of neighbours on the street just up and left without so much as a by-your-leave and under as yet unknown circumstances. I have seen the way that magnificent catalpa tree on a neighbour's front lawn holds my attention each time I walk under it, as do the red willow roots glistening, like cords of red licorice, in the creek whose meandering path we can follow across the length of the neighbourhood, till it merges with the gentle currents of the Grand River. I saw the time, during the pandemic, when the whole world was in lockdown and there was nothing to do but roam our streets and talk to our neighbours, albeit with six feet of pavement between us; when we learnt that as socially distanced as we were, we had never been so connected to the people who lived nearest to us, the people who, be it masked or unmasked, shared our hopes and fears, breathed our air.

The terrain that is our home amounts to a quarter-acre property, which sits at the eastern flank of Colonial Acres, a residential neighbourhood so named not in celebration of the city's settler-colonial history, as I once thought, but in a land developer's love of the symmetrical lines and rectangular shapes of Colonial Revival New England architecture, which sort of adds up to another kind of celebration of pioneer identity.[6] At least this was the template Charles Voelker, a local architect and politician nicknamed "Colonial Charlie," had wished to reproduce in Waterloo, a city largely built by German-speaking Mennonites who began to leave Pennsylvania in the late eighteenth century, many of them pacifists

The Land That Is

fleeing persecution for refusing to take up arms during the American Revolution. They travelled upwards of twenty-five kilometres a day in Conestoga wagons, found their way to the northern shores of Lake Erie and beyond, moving steadily up the Grand River, finding safe passage along a trail system already marked out and long-since travelled by the Mississauga people.[7]

Is it in the knowledge of land-lore, historical and local, that I start to see, really see, *the land that is*? Knowing that the Waterloo township was so named in 1816, replacing its pecuniary designation as "Block Number Two," when it was valued as little more than hectares of wilderness parcelled out to farmers with names like Schneider, Weber, Brubacher and Eby.[8] Knowing that this neighbourhood at the northeastern perimeter of the city was built on farmland once owned by a handful of agriculturalists might explain why an old apple tree down the street sits somewhere between public and private property, a testament to the orchards that once were, its scaffolded boughs overladen with fruit that no one seems to pick. It also points to some of the contradictions of this land, where a river that once helped define treaty territory and early settlement patterns is singularly absent in this city's urban schema and cultural psyche. It's almost as if the "people more often turned their backs on the Grand River,"[9] local historian Elizabeth Bloomfield declares, as seemingly mystified as I have been by this geographic oversight. Or knowing that the river came to be regarded as a utilitarian thing, be it as a water resource for settler-farmers or as a dumping ground for settler-industrialists, and so the city grew around field boundaries and factories, rather than the river that ran through it, deeper and longer than any highway artery.

Whatever the reason, this peculiar disregard for the Grand River, at least in this small stretch of its journey southward to Lake Erie, is itself a defining feature of the riverine *land that is* – one that makes our own proximity to the river another kind of insider knowledge. Of course, we can only access it in short, discontinuous trails, but there is comfort in knowing that the river is a mere twelve-minute walk from our doorstep, close enough that we even had the pleasure of hosting a mink (or maybe a muskrat?) in a shallow lake formed in the depression of our lawn during a particularly vigorous spring thaw. Close enough to watch the geese fly overhead and imagine them holding a conference on the river's shallow outcroppings. Close enough to track the grasses, native and non-native (cattails and phragmites), flowering plants (euphorbia, dame's rocket, marsh marigold), trees (those ubiquitous weeping willows with their glistening red roots) and shrubs (highbush cranberry, staghorn

sumac, red osier dogwood) growing along the creek and all the way down to the riverbanks. Close enough to take in the wonder of a frozen river, its course still running, albeit unseen, below jagged sheets of ice stained in hues of celestial blue, as if heavenly spirits spilled a pot of indigo ink while carving their initials on a cloud.

Knowing that a small bungalow on our street once belonged to one of the many war veterans to whom this land was, once again, parcelled out as part of the Veterans' Land Act in 1957 also tells me something about *the land that is*, like why some of the streets have names like Normandy Avenue. It helps explain why many of us now have quarter-acre properties, four equally proportioned segments of the one-acre properties intended for this type of "victory-housing" (a low-budget, compact architectural style characteristic of post-WWII housing). Knowing that one of these war veterans, by all accounts a "crotchety old guy," got the lone streetlight erected here because he objected to young couples using the foot of his driveway as "make-out alley" is a nugget of an anecdote shared during one of those pandemic encounters with a dear neighbour.[10] Such anecdotes may amount to little more than neighbourly gossip, but they put my ear to this ground, making me privy to the stories it has to tell. And knowing pieces of trivia that even some of my neighbours may not know – like the fact that a field at the heart of our neighbourhood used for the occasional baseball game and, increasingly, soccer practice was once an airstrip for a private flight school called the Kitchener-Waterloo Flying Club (operating from the 1930s to 1951, when it was dismantled) – makes me think that I, too, can be in possession of the kind of knowledge that makes a local a local, a denizen a citizen, an outsider an insider.

These small things I know, but as someone who has come to gardens and gardening later in life, there is so much more I have as yet to learn about this land. I want to know which trees were uprooted and what kind of flora and fauna were displaced to make room for cities like Waterloo. I want to know what this street, this borough, this northeastern edge of a city's limits, buffered by cornfields, looked like before my arrival. Are the roses and hostas and lanky Jack pines growing in our garden an accurate portrait of the land before Colonial Acres was built, or before the war veterans moved in, or before the farmers planted apple orchards and sugar beets or cleared entire deciduous forests of everything but the sugar maple, tapping with unquenchable thirst its liquid gold?[11]

Garden Inventories

If I really hope to figure out what it means to be rooted to a place, perhaps I need to step out of our garden. I should expand the field of study, like venturing into the Colonial Creek Link that runs the length of our neighbourhood and empties out into the Grand River. Or into the conservation areas or woodlands that lie five thousand Fitbit steps from our house. And perhaps I might even have to follow my neighbours into places like the Kawarthas, Muskokas and Grey and Bruce counties (also known as Ontario's much-touted cottage country), where settlers have been communing with this land for centuries, and Indigenous peoples, for millennia – long, long, long before Ronaldo and I ever got here. That place where locals go to commune with the land outside their own backyards might tell me something about how familial and cultural lore is shaped by this land, or how this land is shaped by familial and cultural lore. There's something to be learned from the anthropology of cottage life, even something to emulate in this perennial desire to leave urbanity behind and retreat into the country's hinterlands. Are these traditions to be wholeheartedly embraced by émigré-settlers in our own evolving relationship to place? Where does tradition risk sliding back into older stories of dispossession and displacement?

This micro-universe that is my garden is a sometimes natural, sometimes wholly unnatural extension of my neighbourhood. Of this land. Most certainly a garden in the making where I become preoccupied, from time to time, with questions about image: In whose image am I making this garden? When not looking at *the lands that were*, dare I sneak peeks at, even strive to imitate, the kinds of gardens my neighbours grow? I strap on my walking shoes

The Land That Is

and put my ear to the ground in an effort to look and to listen. Like the manicured lawn or the sights and sounds of a fleeting summer season, what will these gardens have to say about the class constructs, cultural preoccupations and social mores of this land? Do the things we prize in our gardens here, like imported varieties of the hybrid tea rose, have native corollaries? Why do so many fruit trees in  this suburban landscape, like the cherry tree under which my mother and my father-in-law lay buried, not yield fruit? Why do all these "non-fruiting varieties" rub me the wrong way, and send me into pitiful bouts of nostalgia for other lands where gardens teeming with flower *and* fruit are, in the cultural if not also the spiritual imagination, looked upon as a veritable paradise on earth?

These questions keep hurling me back to *the lands that were*. To the vaguest memory of a garden in Karachi, Pakistan, where the first five years of my life were lived. A garden emblematized by a tree known as the champa (a native variety of magnolia), simply because I have a picture of my four-year-old self sitting in the sculptural embrace of our mum's beloved tree. Or yet another garden in England where a crescent-shaped rose bed takes centre stage in my childhood memories of idyllic country landscapes. Or a distinctly tropical slice – more like a sliver – of a garden in the urban sprawl of Manila, Philippines, where, with or without the luxury of a garden, the air was filled with insect orchestras and even the most urban vista might be punctuated with coconut and papaya palms.

But here, in *the land that is*, desert sand has turned to snow. Mango trees have turned to sugar maples. Monsoon winds from the Arabian Sea or equatorial trade winds from the Pacific Ocean are stopped dead in their tracks by Arctic air, an Atlantic gale, a polar vortex, telling us we have landed on foreign soil – on the other side of a gash where even the Earth's axis has shifted by degrees. As newcomers to this land, we spend much of our time hobbling about like newborns learning to walk with anxious, hesitant eyes because, for all we know, we may be spit out and hurled into the Earth's orbit again. Perhaps, for this reason, I don't recall my parents ever concerning themselves with the geography that is Canada – with the land, landscape, that sort of thing – save for immediate challenges such as resetting our bodies and minds to the seasonal rhythms of a northern climate. Needless to say, this alone is no small feat for those born in places where there are only two seasons – dry and hot or wet and hot – and where winters involve little more than the donning of a Kashmiri shawl. For the recently arrived immigrant the business of survival is paramount. We're so preoccupied with putting one foot in front of the other that we can't see the forest for the trees, especially because this forest – deciduous, boreal, Carolinian – looks a bit unreal. Like it's been torn from the pages of a *National Geographic* for people more accustomed to other kinds of forests – arid, temperate, tropical.

When my family cleared – anxious, grateful and exhausted – Canadian customs at the Halifax International Airport on a deceptively chilly June afternoon in 1987, we had no friends or

The Land That Is

family to greet us on our arrival, and relied on taxis to transport us and our oversized luggage to a hotel in downtown Halifax. Our day of arrival is obscured by a jet-lagged, displaced persons' haze, save for that forty-minute taxi ride from airport to hotel. I can see the back of our driver's platinum-blond hair. I can see her peering eyes in the rear-view mirror, stealing glimpses of my brother and myself, two passengers slumped over in the back of her sedan, far too young to look so world-weary, the intrepid wind in their adolescent sails at least momentarily knocked out of them. I can hear the "hard rock" station blaring out of car speakers like a jolt of adrenalin shocking us out of our time-zone-shifting stupor. But more than all this, I see a moving landscape of uninterrupted, indiscernible green. The blond hair, the hard rock, the unfamiliar chill of a bright sunny day – none of this awakens me to the newness and strangeness of Canada quite like that evergreen forest. I detect nothing in this landscape that registers as home, and a curiosity mildly piqued instantly turns to the émigré's affliction: the desire to look back and yearn for the land left behind, for *the lands that were*.

But with time – seventeen years and counting, to be precise – I have come to distinguish in that opaque wall of green variegated shades of black spruce, eastern hemlock, balsam fir. And then a flash of mottled white bark punching through the forest canopy alerts me to aspens and birch, the exclamation marks of the Acadian and, more broadly, boreal forest. With time, I start to learn to love *the land that is* on its own terms, but also in the space of memory, and I recall a trip to northern Pakistan, where evergreens, including varieties of fir, spruce, cedar and pine, are as "at home" in the Swat Valley of the Hindu Kush as they are along the concrete highways, rugged shorelines and hinterlands of Canada. I start to see that *the lands that were* and *the land that is* are not quite so alien to each other, after all. In fact, *the land that is* can sometimes read like a botanist's ledger of *the lands that were*, because plants migrate with people, cross borders, become "naturalized," find their place, be it in harmony with or to the detriment of the new land. I arrive, in other words, at a place of sustained looking that is neither wholly distorted by memories of *the lands that were* nor unduly eclipsed by *the land that is*.

States of arrival, like states of rootedness and belonging, do not begin and end at a customs checkpoint. More often, they emerge over time, and bear no expiry date. They grow in the spaces we create and curate for ourselves, like this little square pocket of land that is our garden. Ideally, they are nurtured in the space of interrelation, not just in our neighbourhoods or communities filled with people as diverse as ourselves, but also through our active acquaintance with our natural environment. Our acquaintance with such things as the lanky Jack pines, which, in our seventeenth year in this home, have signalled the end of their own relatively short life cycle. Our acquaintance with the eastern white pines Ronaldo planted to replace our little Jack pine forest, a gesture which now seems all the more significant in our awareness that, in the Grand River region, the eastern white pine is the Tree of Peace (Ohnehta'kowa in the Mohawk language), symbolizing the unification of the Haudenosaunee peoples of the Six Nations.[12] And even our acquaintance with the smallest of things, like the indelible dandelion carpeting our gardens and streetscapes to the ardent pleasure of pollinating insects and the zealous contempt of lawn-worshipers across the great length and breadth of this land.

Contrapuntal Gardeners

Ronaldo and I moved to Waterloo from Montreal, where we lived a distinctly urban life, our green thumbs applied only to tropical houseplants. Our move from Quebec to Ontario was necessarily a more modest migration than the uprooting we had experienced as young adults, but our interprovincial migration is proving to be no less of an education, especially for novice gardeners eager to put down roots, a seemingly natural antidote to our multiple uprootings. Like the garden-building Mughals who arrived in the Indian subcontinent from the Central Asian plains, I was a newcomer to the land in which I was to tend my first garden. This land turned out to be little more than the equivalent of a flower bed or a water feature in the Mughals' iconic gardens.

Ronaldo and I would be classified as the 1.5 generation, dependents of the first-generation immigrant under whose wing we left our respective homelands, but still old enough to carry that land with us, in our memories, if not also in our hearts. For those who still remember, migration yields the curious state of finding oneself simultaneously aware of two lands or, more deeply, one's lived experience in more than one land. This is what Palestinian theorist Edward Said refers to as the "contrapuntal vision" of the displaced – where lived experiences of different geographies or different lands coexist in counterpoint, each one unique but interdependent. This state of awareness might, at first, create dissonance or disharmony, each land competing with the other for primacy of vision. But much like two overlaid lines (or counterpoints) of music in a Bach piano concerto (or even the more ambitious pop song), we can also experience them contrapuntally, as a single harmonious melody.[1]

In gardening terms, my own "contrapuntal vision" is refracted through multiple and distinct geographies. The gardens of my infancy were in the hot coastal Karachi plains, where fruit trees such as chikoo, guava and mulberry were a child's sugary paradise; a later childhood was spent trailing my mother around English country gardens with rose bushes, sour cherries, strawberry patches and apple trees. In my teen years I was enamoured by the tropical landscapes of the Philippines, a place where those very same apples (i.e., North American varieties such as Granny Smith or Red Delicious) were an exotic luxury item imported to satisfy the nostalgic palates of American military personnel. Our home in a Manila suburb was also where I witnessed a scraggly papaya tree uprooted in a hurricane fly past our window, reminding me that gardens, even walled ones like Sikandra, built by the third Mughal emperor Akbar (1542–1605), are always an extension of their wider natural environment, each one subject to the other's flights of fancy.[2]

The common denominator for me, at least, in these contrapuntal landscapes is the central figure of the fruit tree. And in this I am not alone: Ronaldo's memories of those lands left behind are similarly imbued by fruit trees. No garden, even those we create in our mind's eye, seems complete without a fruit tree, so something seemed terribly amiss in the garden we inherited from the previous owner of our Waterloo home. This garden had a few striking features, one of which used to come in handy whenever directions were called for: "Just look for the only house on the street dotted with Jack pines!" But fruit trees only stood out in their absence, so we decided to make the first tree we planted in this garden an apple of the gala variety. It seemed like a safe bet given that we live a stone-fruit's throw from Martin's Family Fruit Farm, one of the largest apple growers in Ontario. As their website plainly puts it, "We're All About Apples," even though the Martins' extensive orchards first came about as a seed of an idea sown by a family acquaintance from Yugoslavia.[3] In other words, the apples consumed in this region are another denizen in Canada, like the Mennonite farmers who cultivate them, and the Pakistani Pirbhais and Guatemalan Garcias who happily consume them.

In fact, apple trees, like pears, peaches and cherries, can be thought of as "Asian" transplants, or fruits with Central Asian provenance – the original home of the founding Mughal emperor, Zahiruddin Muhammad Babur (1483–1530) – where cool nights and variable climes make for ideal growing conditions. Babur's fondness for fruits travelled with him to the Indian subcontinent, a land with its own diversity of fruits, including several dozen varieties of mango. Like the US personnel at the Clark and Subic Bay military bases in Manila, however, it was the apple the homesick emperor longed for in his alien surroundings. From Central Asia, the apple travelled westward and farther eastward, proving to be highly adaptive to the European climate, where it came to be renamed "æppel" in Old English. Since the seventeenth century, it has been a staple in the North American diet, eventually giving rise to the "national apple of Canada," the McIntosh, discovered and then cultivated on John McIntosh's Ontario farm in 1811.[4]

I feel a certain kinship to the apple now, not only considering its Asian origin story, but also because of its cross-cultural provenance. But my social conditioning was such that I considered apples a quintessentially European fruit, and my Asian side still yearned for a tree that recalled those other more distinctly tropical or even arid garden-scapes of childhood – that is, I hankered after fruiting trees that spoke to my own equatorial sensibility.

Like all immigrants to Canada, we learned quite soon after moving here that the weather is a national obsession, and with good reason. The climate is so varied and so changeable that we live in a land not of weather forecasts but of "weather stories," a charming expression used by local meteorologists. Transplanting ourselves to Waterloo from Montreal made us aware of yet more "weather stories." For one, there was a notable difference in snowfall accumulation between southern Quebec and southern Ontario. Just to put this into gardening terms, while both regions lie along the Great Lakes St. Lawrence Lowlands, Montreal's "plant hardiness zone" lies at least one notch below that of Toronto and Waterloo, making it a far more difficult beast to tame.

This was a lesson learned the first time I visited the home of my mother-in-law, Rebeca Gonzalez, and her little plot of land in quartier Saint-Michel, just north of the Trans-Canada Highway, which cuts through Montreal Island like a concrete version of the mighty St. Lawrence River. In my mother-in-law's garden (seen in the next two images), it was Ronaldo who flexed his muscles with axe, hoe, shovel and rake, turning clayish soil into an arable vegetable plot, which he would churn and turn before and at the end of every planting season. On one side of his mother's garden, Ronaldo had erected a massive arbour for her prized beans. Below this lay an outcropping of the largest zucchinis and squashes I had ever set my eyes on. At the end of the garden also stood a few noble stalks of corn. As I would come to discover through my newly acquired Latin American family, these three crops, which are  always planted together, are staples in Guatemalan cuisine, and even sacred staples in Mayan lore. The tall, sturdy cornstalks stand in as a natural trellis for the wayward bean vines, and the squash maps out a carpet of leaves and tendrils that function as a natural weed killer. More recently, I came to learn that it is this same triad of crops – beans, squash and corn – that the Ojibwe and other First Nations peoples refer to as "the Three Sisters," attesting to the trade links and other cross-cultural influences between the Indigenous Peoples of the American hemisphere.

Rebeca's garden consisted of a well-tended vegetable plot on one side, and a bed of wildflowers on the other. The latter was thanks to Ronaldo (pictured on the next page), who would often gift his mother wildflower seeds, including poppies, mallows and sunflowers. Rebeca had a rather strong dislike for trees planted too close to a house – more a personal phobia than a cultural mindset

Garden Inventories

— so there were no fruit trees in her garden. However, Ronaldo informed me that their family's urban yard in Guatemala City did

have several fruit trees; in fact, he had even managed to reproduce a sliver of this childhood memory by growing a lemon tree from seed, where it once filled his apartment with eternal sunshine. I must confess that I always struggled with Rebeca's treeless lot, though, to be fair, I now see that even one tree on that small plot of land would have created a shade garden, anathema to "the Three Sisters" who thrive on "full sun" in the mercilessly brief growing period their climate affords them. With or without trees, then, this garden's purpose was to bear fruit, at least in the figurative sense.

"To bear fruit," as the *Cambridge Learner's Dictionary* tells us, is to produce a "successful" outcome.[5] The *American Heritage Dictionary of Idioms* states the expression "to bear fruit," implying "to yield results," came about in 1879.[6] For isn't a tree laden with fruit a successful yield? A mark of success? And isn't such a mark of success a thing of beauty in its own right? Maybe even a heavenly recompense? Early colonial settlers certainly thought so. In the nineteenth century, Samuel Strickland, the brother of renowned writers Susanna Moodie and Catharine Parr Traill, advised "the emigrant, who becomes an agriculturalist, to pay great attention

Contrapuntal Gardeners

to orchard planting."[7] In this vein, we might need to look back to our gardeners of yore – those early settlers for whom "fruit growing was so important . . . [that] almost half of the 390 pages in Beadle's *Canadian Fruit, Flower, and Kitchen Gardener* are devoted to the 'Fruit Garden.'"[8]

About four-hundred-odd years before the Stricklands planted their orchards in Upper Canada another breed of immigrant was starting to settle another kind of harsh, indifferent terrain: namely, the hot, dusty plains and hills of the Indian subcontinent. These settlers, colonizers in their own right, extolled the virtues of the ornamental garden and orchard alike. In fact, they not only extolled a garden's virtues but also subscribed to a garden philosophy with religious devotion. These settlers, a sturdy folk hailing from the Central Asian plains, came to establish one of the most refined garden civilizations in human history. This was the Mughal Empire established in 1526 across much of the Indian subcontinent. As an Islamic civilization, the Mughals were schooled in Islamic principles, the first of which was "the abundant fruits" to be enjoyed in the afterlife.

I was five when my family left Pakistan, at which point we embarked on a circuitous journey to England, the United Arab Emirates, the Philippines and, finally, Canada, so my influences are as varied and discontinuous as they are embedded in my parents' individual sensibilities, which were at times the only constant in our travels from continent to continent. My parents (both now deceased) were born in pre-Partition India: my mother in Uttar Pradesh (also home to Agra's most famous Mughal landmark, the Taj Mahal), and my father in Gujarat, in the city of Mumbai. Historic upheavals and subsequent migrations only deepened my father's passion for the fruits and foods of the East, and only compelled my mother to further dig in her heels in the gardens she nurtured in each of her homes. These two sensibilities combined have much to do with my own interest in how foods and plants (and of course people) travel.

My parents' fondness for food and for gardening took root in their natal lands, steeped in the legacies of the Mughal Empire. My maternal grandfather, the son of a nawab (roughly the equivalent of an English lord), was among the last in that dwindling and, by the early twentieth century, largely landless (and, much like those English lords, bankrupt) cohort of Mughal aristocracy, but I like to think of my mother's green thumb as genetic residue from her horticulturally minded ancestors. As I look back on a collection of old family slides from the late sixties and early seventies, I notice a pattern: most of the pictures of Mum were taken outdoors, in her own or someone else's garden. Here she is in Karachi, Pakistan, her fingers gently tugging a banana tree frond, which I presume she must have been admiring or inspecting, as is the gardener's habit. My father's family were of a more business-minded merchant class, but I would surmise that his curiosity and passion for new spices, foods and culinary traditions is similarly rooted in the

Mughal heritage. The Mughal emperors, from Babur to Bahadur Shah, indelibly transformed the palates and landscapes of the region. The fragrant and spice-tiered biryani, the beloved South Asian rice dish likely inspired by the Persian birian, epitomizes Mughal appetites for culinary experimentation. And the gardens of the Ram Bagh (Babur's first garden, in Agra), the Shalimar Bagh and the Taj Mahal, remind us that horticulture itself was elevated to new heights under Mughal rule in the Indian subcontinent. Though each of the Mughal emperors were invested in gardening to varying degrees, the sacred nature of the garden was a principle shared across the Mughal line. So much so that Emperor Akbar's tomb, which sits at the heart of Sikandra, in the historic seat of Mughal power, bears the inscription *These are the gardens of Eden; enter them to dwell therein eternally.*

Paradise, or Jannah (*garden* in Arabic), awaits the faithful in the form of a glorious garden of verdant green, flowing water and sensuous fruits. That Jannah is a fruit-bearing garden is one of the sacred tenets of Islam, found in the Surah al-Waqi'ah, the Quranic verses relating to the afterlife: "Allah hath promised to Believers, men and women, gardens under which rivers flow, to dwell therein, and beautiful mansions in gardens of everlasting bliss."[9] The verses also include references to a variety of fruits, including palms, pomegranates, bananas and grapes, as well as trees we might today classify as ornamental. And so it goes, those admitted to the garden will be among "trees with thorns removed / And trees layered with fruit / And shade extended / And water poured out / And fruit abundant and varied."[10]

So valorized is the "fruit abundant" of Jannah that the Mughal emperors who ruled much of the Indian subcontinent from the sixteenth to nineteenth centuries would reserve entire sections of their magnificent gardens for orchards planted in meticulous designs, such as the Charbagh depicted in Mughal paintings.[11] Adapted

Garden Inventories

from Persian models to suit the Indian climate and topography, the Charbagh (in Urdu, *char* is the number four, and in Farsi, *bagh* is *garden*) is a quadrilateral garden design, irrigated by water channels, adorned and harmonized with Mughal architecture, and at the centre of which lies an impressive water feature. The four quadrants were reserved for distinctive planting functions – including the bustan or fruit garden, and gulistan or floral garden – filled with native and non-native specimens. In the case of the fruit garden, pear, apple, peach, date, almond, fig and mulberry were among some of the fruits to have been enjoyed there.[12] The following image catalogued in Babur's illustrated memoir, the *Baburnama*, best captures the Charbagh's elaborate design.

Contrapuntal Gardeners

When our freshly planted gala apple tree was mistaken for a rabbit's feast during a particularly harsh winter, I mourned its premature loss, and tried not to victim blame the starving rabbit. Then, like Babur and his troops (or, really, more like my intrepid mother), I shook off the gardener's blues, laced up my sneakers and set off on exploratory missions around my neighbourhood for some local horticultural inspiration. These suburban front gardens – I bristle at the more colloquial term *yard*, which conjures barren lots where used cars and radiating computer parts go to die – are often punctuated with statuesque centrepiece trees like blue spruce and silver maple. But "curb appeal" and "fruit trees" are rarely synonymous here – that is, unless you come across those most paradoxical of beasts: ornamental "non-fruiting" fruit trees, such as crabapple and cherry, engineered to produce magnificent but entirely sterile spring blossoms. Within this genus of non-fruiting fruit trees, another curious specimen caught my eye: the dwarf ornamental whose daintiness bespoke years of slavish pruning. Among these oddities was a tree that looked vaguely familiar, in that tropical kind of way. If nothing else, I appreciated how this particular tree branched up and out and sideways, taking idiosyncratic meanderings along driveways and garden paths.

The tree that caught my eye was a weeping mulberry. Not only did it have character and an indomitable spirit, resisting some of the more regimented aspects of suburban landscaping, it was, more significantly, a fruit-bearing tree. The mulberry was a tree of my childhood – one that took me back, like the mythical apple of Eden, to our first garden. To a home in Karachi. To roots. Let's just say, the first time I bit into a juicy mulberry ripened on our very own tree in Waterloo, I recovered a taste of my Pakistani childhood. I also recovered a word: *shatut*.

Garden Inventories

☙

Shatut, aka *shahtoot*. A hybrid developed in Pakistan: a *Morus nigra* hybrid, a black mulberry. *Shatut* is a Farsi word. *Shah* translates as *king*, thus disclosing its Persian origins; *tut*, also spelled *toot*, refers to the berry. A Wikipedia search for *shatut* may land you in a village in the Khorasan province of Iran. It may also land you in a picturesque township in the Himalayan foothills. Both Iran and the Himalayan regions of China appear as points of origin for the black Pakistan mulberry. Like the red mulberry, the black mulberry is a large, fast-growing tree. It can reach sixty to eighty feet in height. So there we have it: the king's mulberry or king mulberry – a royal fruit, certainly, given its massive size (the berry can be as long as four inches) and its unrivalled sweetness. In the Indian state of Gujarat, there is evidence suggesting some Mughal gardens were exclusively devoted to the mulberry but these were eventually converted to farmlands in more recent times.[13]

My brother, Reza, fondly recalls a giant shatut tree at my paternal grandmother's house in Karachi. It was the pride of the household, he tells me. With childlike glee, he adds, "I remember climbing it to get the fruit. And the driveway and patio would be splattered with fallen fruit when in season, like bloodstains on the white patio tiles. The harvest would also be distributed among the family, a special treat!"[14] On this side of the planet, the shatut, aka the Pakistan mulberry, is a rarity that appears to be seducing avid tree growers in the southern United States, where it has a better chance of survival. Onegreenworld, a commercial supplier specializing in "unique plants, shrubs and trees," hails the Pakistan mulberry as yielding the "worlds [sic] largest Mulberry fruit," and goes on to describe the fruits as "so elongated they are almost bizarre looking and sure to wow your friends!"[15] As for "tasting is believing," this may be an impossibility so far from Pakistani soil, though I can attest to the fact that mulberry varieties, even those grown in North America, have one thing in common: they are honey-sweet and possess none of the tartness associated with brambleberries, such as the blackberry, which they most closely resemble.

While I was reconciled to the idea of not being able to replicate my shatut-eating childhood in the colder Canadian climate, I was not prepared for just how hard it would be to find a fruiting mulberry of *any* variety at our local nurseries. Upon closer inspection, I realized that some, if not most, of the mulberry trees planted in my neighbours' gardens did not produce fruits, and were selected for precisely such a characteristic: namely, to be non-fruiting. The idea of selecting a non-fruiting variety of a fruit tree was baffling for someone hailing from an environment where fruiting trees would take pride of place in the garden. Was I actually going against the grain in setting out to plant a fruiting mulberry? If so, how had the idea of ornamentation taken us so far from the raison d'être of plants and plant life: that is, to bear fruit? How have we arrived at a place where edibles, like kale and cabbage, are planted for mere ornamentation while fruiting trees are regarded with suspicion? How was my own contrapuntal perspective colouring my gardening practices?

Since it was the non-fruiting mulberry that prompted these questions, it seemed likely that this variety of tree held some of my answers. To begin, I learned that the white mulberry, or *Morus alba*, we commonly see in their dwarfed, weeping forms in Ontario gardens is a "non-native" species. *Morus alba* was brought to the United States in the 1800s for its commercial properties in sericulture, or the production of silk devised and cultivated as a millennia-old practice in China. The white mulberry held the secret to sericulture since silk worms love to feast on its leaves. Hoping to succeed where the British had failed several centuries earlier, sericulture nonetheless proved as inimitable to American agriculturalists as it did to James I and his successors.[16] The mulberry's early commercial usage suggests that it may never have enjoyed a reputation in colonial North America as a fruiting tree. However, like ornamental gardening practices, the white mulberry had taken root and it was here to stay.

The mulberry seen in its weeping form in my neighbours' gardens is, in fact, an expression of ever-changing gardening practices and tastes as much as it is a product of history. But I didn't realize just how much so till I spoke to Jon L. Peter, curator and manager of Plant Records at Ontario's Royal Botanical Gardens, who explained that the weeping variety of the white mulberry commonly planted in Ontario gardens are asexually propagated male clones. The *Morus alba* 'pendula,' aka the weeping mulberry, is usually top grafted onto *Morus alba* var. *tartarica* rootstock. These trees have long histories of selection and hybridization, such that the white mulberry, like the apple, is far from a simple transplant, boasting as it does a complex and dynamic provenance. Indeed, the white mulberry rootstock, the *Morus alba* var. *tartarica*, is itself a more recent Russian import, which means that the humble mulberry may have yet another branch in its botanical lineage.[17]

Sadly, in true Darwinian vigour, the white mulberry's longevity has also come about at the expense of its native counterpart, the red mulberry. The *Morus alba* has the potential for the graft union to fail, the scion to fail and/or for the rootstock to take over, which makes this variety potentially invasive. The introduction of this non-native variety has proven detrimental to the red mulberry, the only variety of its kind native to Canada. Tragically, the *Morus rubra* is now classified as SAR, or species at risk, largely because of its hybridization with the imported white mulberry.

When I asked Jon why the local nursery industry seems to favour the non-fruiting variety of the mulberry, he informed me that the female clones were deemed undesirable in the nursery and garden trade on account of their "messy fruits." Having no expertise in this area, the mention of male versus female clones prompted further investigation, for which I consulted Dr. David Galbraith, head of science at the Royal Botanical Gardens.[18] As I learned from Dr. Galbraith, there are "dioecious" (Greek for "two households") and "monoecious" species in the plant world – the former possessing either a single sex in the form of male or female flowers and the latter possessing both male and female flowers. This helped put Jon's comment about the "undesirable" female clones into some perspective: the female tree bears ovaries and is fruit-bearing, whereas the male tree only bears pollen. It came as some assurance that many fruit trees are inherently male, or non-fruiting, which meant that the non-fruiting tree is not, as I first imagined, a bioengineered monstrosity so much as a naturally occurring phenomenon: This seemed to make the idea of a non-fruiting mulberry a tad more palatable. Almost, but not quite.

The *Morus alba* 'pendula' or weeping mulberry we commonly see in our neighbours' gardens is, indeed, a male non-fruiting clone, but let's not be fooled by its shrinking demeanour, because it is here by design. It is the dominant variety by virtue of human machinations! Its counterpart, the fruiting mulberry, has been exiled to the sidelines. Perhaps the vilification of the fruiting female clone is better likened to a woman's menstrual cycle, an object of shame signifying the loss of virginal purity given its tendency to sully our pristine lawns – remember those "bloodstains on the white patio tiles" – turning it into a woeful, brandished thing. In North Carolina, charges against this fruiting tree, labelled the "problem child," are numerous;[19] closer to home, the DeGroot's Nurseries in Sarnia, Ontario, dedicates a colourful feature on the mulberry's various pitfalls:

> Watch where you walk. Fallen Mulberry fruit will turn your concrete driveway into a black mess and can be as slippery as a banana peel on the shop room floor. . . .
> . . . Nobody plants Mulberries. They sprout up innocently but, in a few years, become too difficult to remove or dig up. . . .
> Mulberries attract birds which may be a nuisance for those with white driveways and polished cars. As fruit turns from green to white to red to black, so does the colour of bird droppings. . . .
> When Mulberry fruit ripens to its reddish black colour it eventually drops leaving a smelly sticky mess that attract a variety of insects, most of which are bothersome houseflies.[20]

Perhaps the white mulberry's disrepute does not rest entirely on the shoulders of the North American nursery industry. After all, it was Shakespeare and, before him, the Roman poet Ovid who could be said to have sullied the mulberry's good name in *A Midsummer Night's Dream* and *Metamorphoses* respectively.[21] Just think of Pyramus, that proverbial star-crossed lover who, in a comic twist of fate, takes his own life under a mulberry tree: "And Thisbe, tarrying in mulberry shade, / His dagger drew, and died."[22] In fact, it is Pyramus's blood that splatters across the hanging fruit of the white mulberry, forever staining it a blood-clot red. However, as Shakespeareans might argue, reading the Bard's comedies without the tragedies is like a Pyramus without a Thisbe . . . or, dare I say, a male mulberry without a female mulberry! For it is in the tragedy of *Coriolanus* that a mother urges her son to soften his approach in matters of diplomacy, taking her cue from the mulberry's delicate-natured countenance: "Now humble as the ripest mulberry / That will not hold the handling."[23] Alas, the mulberry's illustrious past, figurative and other, seems lost on those fixated with its more "problematic" nature, suggesting the extent to which myths and legends govern our natural world. Indeed, many would argue that even the gender classifications we impose on the natural world are somewhat spurious.

Even so, the North Carolinian warning persists: those who wish to plant the white mulberry, "be aware!" The message has spread from the southern United States to southern Ontario. At our local nursery, my husband and I were encouraged to purchase the non-fruiting mulberry and, like that precocious child in the sandbox, I threw a horticultural tantrum, insisting that we wanted the fruiting mulberry because, of course, what in God's name was the point of buying a fruit tree that bore no fruit!

Our beloved weeping mulberry, freakishly alone in a grove of non-fruiting mulberries, came home with us, where it now grows, not by the driveway, all boxed in and neutered, but in the back garden where it sits happily unfettered in our direct line of vision. And so it is the problem child, the tragic symbol, the elusive fruit of this fruiting tree that got me thinking about the topsy-turviness of our gardening practices, where edibles are rendered inedible, even wholly undesirable, in the world of ornamentals. The mulberry tree has made itself at home in our garden for the last eight years. It is, in the final verdict, achingly slow-growing, especially compared to the shatut of my childhood, though perhaps that is just the nature of its now selectively dwarfed profile. But it has never failed to yield results. Every year around mid-July, I anticipate a bountiful harvest but am disappointed to find the tree virtually devoid of fruit, not because of some nefarious horticulturist plot, but because the local fauna is just as enamoured with this fruit as I am. In fact, the cardinals and squirrels start devouring the berries long before they have a chance to ripen, much less fall to the ground. Last year, a groundhog took up residence somewhere in our garden, and it did not take him long to discover the gastronomical rewards to be had – in both the vine-like foliage and ripening berries – of our weeping mulberry. I woke up one morning to see him sitting at the crown of our beloved mulberry, perched like a Mughal emperor atop his courtly throne, supreme purveyor of his very own pleasure garden! In our garden it would seem the tree doesn't even have the opportunity to live up to its ill repute as a mess-making problem child, because it is picked clean long before such unforgivable sins as a fruit-strewn lawn can occur!

In the process of writing this piece, I revisited our local nursery to remind myself of the various descriptors and classifications of the *Morus alba* 'pendula.' In research terms I came up short, because there was no literature to be found on the tree except the vague notification that it is "no longer available." Tastes and trends are fickle and in constant flux so the white mulberry has, perhaps, fallen out of favour for good. The more optimistic part of me likes to think that the white mulberry's sudden disappearance from commercial growers' inventories can be attributed to its destructive impact on the native *Morus rubra*, the red mulberry. Like a defective car part recalled to those *yards* where things go to die, this could be a positive sign of conservation efforts to repopulate the native variety.

Contrapuntal Gardeners

The less optimistic part of me thinks that the "buyer-beware" credo has delivered its final blow, leaving all mulberries to Pyramus's tragicomic fate.

Whether the white mulberry lies prostrate in the nursery morgue or is merely undergoing yet more horticultural surgeries, I sincerely hope that this is not the last we have seen of a tree that attests so eloquently to the roots and routes of our intersecting cultural histories. I also hope that whatever tree usurps the mulberry's now centuries-old place in the Canadian garden, the new kid on the block will be afforded the dignity of bearing fruit, be it for human or animal consumption.

In my contrapuntal vision of other lands, other places, other geographies, I am left wondering what Babur and his imperial successors would have done – what divinely inspired punishment they would have meted out – to those harbouring non-fruiting fruit trees or inedible edibles, such as the ornamental kales and cabbages found in city planters, in their paradisiacal gardens. I will just have to wait for the afterlife – the migration to end all migrations, perhaps – to find out.

By Any Other Name

[T]his naming of things is so crucial to possession – a spiritual padlock with the key thrown away – that it is a murder.[1]
– Jamaica Kincaid, "Flowers of Evil"

Princess Margaret.
William Shakespeare.
Mister Lincoln.
Amadeus.
Lady Diana.

A catalogue of roses reads like a guest list for a royal tea party. Some names will wither away, like the weaker cultivars. Others will reign supreme in gardens the world over. But as I work my way through this list, I struggle to find names that tell stories of my own cultural history, as the daughter of South Asian immigrants. And yet, wasn't I the one who came from the continent of the roses – or at least some of the earliest rose cultivars, without which a Princess Margaret or Lady Diana would not smell as sweet?

Names are never neutral. Names hold power. Names have been used in mockery and degradation, a common practice in the Transatlantic Slave Trade. Malcolm X's first act of decolonization was to reject the name imposed on his enslaved ancestors. Names have been wilfully and inadvertently misspelled, mispronounced, distorted and anglicized in the colonial record, where a Pirbhai becomes a Peer-Bhoy; a Mariam, a Mary-Anne. Names have been used to erase entire records of a people's history, culture, religion – you name it.

Mispronunciation can distort a name but we are all guilty of the occasional act of mispronunciation, are we not? Conversely, autocorrect is often responsible for misspelling and misrecognizing names but surely the blame rests squarely on the shoulders of lazy writers who don't take the time to notice. So *Mariam*s turn into *Miriam*s, and I can't begin to count the number of times I've had to explain that in a single letter – a small-case *i* swapped out for a small-case *a* – lies an entire religion, turning an Islamic Mariam into a Hebraic Miriam. Sometimes the *i* is swapped out for a *y*, turning me into a *Maryam* hailing from the Arab-Muslim world rather than a *Mariam* hailing from a set of parents whose trip to Iran made such an impact on them that they returned to Pakistan with a box of pistachios, firoz-encrusted jewellery and, I presume, two popular Irani children's names – Reza and Mariam – for their first two of three children. In my more fanciful moments, I imagine my parents enamoured by the stories and films inspired by the figure of Mariam-uz-Zamani (1542–1623), a Hindu Rajput princess who became Emperor Akbar's third and most favoured wife, affectionately called the Queen Mother because she was the longest reigning Mughal empress. A symbol of interreligious

By Any Other Name

harmony, Mariam-uz-Zamani (erroneously dubbed Jodha Bai by a nineteenth-century British historian), continued to practice, with her husband's blessing, Hindu rites and rituals in the Islamic court; she held her own in matters of state, a voice of considerable political influence, while also building a commercial empire with a fleet of trading ships.[2] And even though *Mariam*, *Miriam* and *Maryam* are all versions of the Biblical Mary (even Mariam-uz-Zamani means Mary of the Age), this neither makes us *Marian*s nor *Mary-Anne*s!

Similarly, when a *Pirbhai* is misnamed a *Pirahbai* (a common misspelling on our utility bills) or a *Per-bay* (a phonetic transcription, I imagine), worlds of history are lost. Let's start with the second part of the name: *bhai*, which means *brother* in Urdu, signalling our mother tongue. *Pir* refers to a Muslim saint or holy person, commonly used for a Sufi saint. Combined, *Pirbhai* means *the brotherhood of the Pir*, or disciples of the saintly religious order, signalling our Islamic heritage and perhaps even some ancestral connection to one of those saintly types. We *Pirbhai*s are often mistaken for Aga Khanis or Ismailis (religious sects of Islam) and it turns out that this is because we, like the followers of these other religious denominations, are ethnically Khojas, a caste of Hindus who were converted to Islam in the fourteenth century by a Persian fellow named Pir Sadr ad-Din (there's that word again: *Pir*). Some of these religious converts became Shiite Muslims, like my father's ancestors; some became Sunni; and some became disciples of the Aga Khan. To add to this ethno-religious cocktail, while Pirbhai is a fairly *un*common name in Pakistan, there seem to be quite a number of Pirbhais in East Africa, most of them émigrés from the Indian subcontinent during the colonial era; thus, while my first name conjures the grand bazaars and Safavid palaces of Iran, my last name conjures nineteenth-century mercantile migrations across the Indian Ocean to places like Zanzibar, Nairobi and Dar es Salaam.[3]

So there is a world of something in a name – a trail of clues that provide insight into history and heritage. To be robbed of a name is to be robbed of both history and heritage. To be robbed, in effect, of story. As an academic specializing in postcolonial literature – that is, literatures produced in response to European imperialism – I am trained to be alert to name-robbing as rigorously as I am trained to be highly suspicious of colonial naming practices. As a gardener in a settler colonial landscape – heck, as a gardener living in a neighbourhood called Colonial Acres – even in the act of selecting plants I am defenceless against the tyranny of names. So why, with all this critical training under my belt, have I been taking the names for local flora, not only in the Canadian landscape but right here, in my own backyard, at face value?

In her books on local flora, such as *Canadian Wild Flowers* (1868) and *Studies of Plant Life in Canada* (1885), amateur botanist Catharine Parr Traill makes special note of the descriptive or "common" names given to native North American plants by early European settlers.[4] Often, these names tell us as much about a plant as the people and culture that named it. In this way, a Juneberry (*Amelanchier*) helpfully signals its fruiting season in late June. In contrast, another common name for this shrub, serviceberry, tells us little about the plant itself. Apparently, New Englanders noted that the ground was sufficiently thawed for grave-digging around the time of the shrub's blooming period, which is how the plant "services" funeral planning. Often, names, both scientific and common, speak to the plant's origin, though some do a better job of this than others. For instance, the Japanese maple in the Canadian landscape makes no bones about *its* point of origin. And nurseries often tag plants with Latin identifiers such as *canadensis*

By Any Other Name

but, as most Canadians know, such wholesale designations do little to capture the zonal and other differences to be found within one province, much less across this vast country.

Canadian horticulturists use botanical taxonomies – at least the scientific ones – from the Carl Linnaeus classification system, which most helpfully provides a common language to organize and study a wide variety of plant life across this planet. But we forget that many of these plants already had names, which are now all but forgotten, if not erased, by this very same system. In a similar vein, Traill showers praise on early settler communities for the enduring names devised for local flora, while perceiving First Nations peoples as an "unlettered society," seemingly incapable of naming things even as they are said to have used a wide range of these very same plants for medicinal or other purposes. I recently learned that under the current rules and regulations of the *International Code of Nomenclature for algae, fungi, and plants*, newly discovered plants, no matter their origin, must be Latinized if they are to be officially recognized by this botanical society.[5] Kind of like the tree falling in the forest, does a plant bearing an Indigenous or non-Western name even exist? Such botanical ledgers thus beg the question: Whose cultural knowledge am I borrowing and reproducing in my garden, and whose cultural knowledge am I burying under this compost heap of names?

The names of our plants matter. Sometimes they help us get to the bottom of why so much of what we plant doesn't quite behave as if it ever belonged here. In looking to my neighbours' gardens or scouring the nurseries for plants and ideas, we develop our own gardens, but in whose image? In whose name? Perhaps I need to rephrase the question: What did these plant names have to tell me about my garden or the natural habitats outside the walls of my garden? What stories did they have to tell? Were they stories of here? Or stories of elsewhere? And what do we lose in erasing Indigenous names for native flora?

The answer, or at least the root of the answer, came to me not in the garden but in the garage, hiding under a piece of discarded Gyproc. It appeared in the form of a rose catalogue, or rather cut-outs from a rose catalogue pinned to the wall in a neat row, like a portrait gallery of patrician stock, with names such as Prince Charles, Mister Lincoln and Queen Elizabeth. Each portrait told a story, and I found myself reading our garage wall like a book of fairy tales. At the centre of this story was an ordinary man named Don – the man who owned this house before we did.

Like most gardeners, Don wanted his little plot of land to say something about him, to reflect his tastes and his vision. Short on gardening know-how, Don had to look elsewhere for inspiration, and where better to turn than to the land of his ancestors, who seemed to know a lot about these things. What would *they* do to turn an ordinary patch into something beautiful – extraordinary, even?

They'd make a proper English garden, of course! I imagine his know-it-all next-door neighbour saying.

And what does that look like? Don called over the fence. But

By Any Other Name

a blizzard was brewing and the neighbour had retreated indoors, where he would hibernate till spring.

A few months later, as the first patch of mouldy grass appeared beneath the melting snow, the mailman, mixing up addresses, stuffed a fancy catalogue filled with glossy images of flowers into Don's mailbox. Don was instantly transported to the land of his ancestors by one special flower appearing, page after page, with colourful names that were vaguely familiar, like Princess Margaret and Charles Darwin. Unable to pick just one of these specimens, he sent off for them all and waited patiently for Queen Victoria's birthday, the public holiday marked for Dons all across this land to set about planting gardens finally safe from the Canadian winter's lethargic farewell. Several months later Don stepped back with pride as the first flower bloomed, and then another and another. The neighbour, who was out mowing his lawn, peeked over the fence, amazed by what he saw. A garden filled with the flowers he had been hoping to order from the catalogue he'd waited all winter long for!

Well, what do you think? Don asked, beaming, but the neighbour kept looking back and forth between his garden and Don's, as if he were taking inventory. Don couldn't help himself and snuck a peek at the neighbour's side of the fence, and sure enough it was also populated with roses, just like his. Granted, his neighbour's garden had neither the number nor variety nor the latest prize-winning specimens Don had ordered from the catalogue, but he spotted a few common ones, like Princess Margaret and hybrid tea.

I planted a proper English garden, just like you said!

But those flowers are supposed to be in my garden! The neighbour shook an accusatory fist.

I beg your pardon! Don had meant to say sorry, but with the roses a slurry of British expressions had planted themselves in his mouth.

You heard me! You've stolen my rose garden!

Okay, so I have used a bit of creative licence to paint a picture of Don's rose fetish. But the part about the rose cut-outs is true. The roses planted around the deck, which we eventually pulled up when the deck was replaced with a stone patio: also true. A sad-looking English rambling rose my husband salvaged and transplanted, before I had any say in it, to a sunny spot where it causes no end of annoyance because it's not only clambering over the fence but also over the apple tree, the flower bed and the two Jack pines it's planted between: true. Don's name: true. Our impression that a plot was afoot, under Don's direction, to turn this piece of land into a facsimile of a proper English garden, because was there ever a flower more synonymous with Englishness than the rose: certifiably true.

The rose. Now there's a flower of considerable standing. Even in its most generic form, the rose reigns supreme for horticulturists and hobby gardeners alike. The genealogy of the cultivated rose is as layered and complex as rose-lore is ubiquitous, in civilizations ancient and contemporary, and across a period of several thousand years. Roses have passed through the thorn-pricked hands of ancient Sumerians, Minoans, Egyptians, Greeks and Romans. As one of the most hybridized species, the quest for a rose cultivar's provenance is, by now, about as fruitless and fraught as, well, any quest for true origin. But let's, for the sake of historical accountability, go back to the time of the Silk Road.

Imagine a caravan of Arab traders galloping on thoroughbred

By Any Other Name

Mongolian horses or seated between the double-humped backs of Bactrian camels. Can you see them approaching your villages and cities all the way from China, as they move stealthily across this globalizing trade route? They come bearing not only eponymous silk but an array of world-altering inventions, from paper to ceramics, as well as perishable goods, like cinnamon and spice and everything nice. These traders are not just conveyors of product, but also of things not so easily quantified, like ideas, knowledge and even inspiration. For when they stumble upon such things as a classical water garden at one of their Persian trading posts, they are instantly bewitched. And what would such a landscape design be without its most essential ingredient: plants. So these traders turn to sea voyages (maybe even on one of Mariam-uz-Zamani's ships!) to transport some of the more perishable items, and we might imagine them hauling seeds and flower cuttings that have a special place in these gardens, like the autumn damask rose, grown not only for its intoxicating scent but also for its distillation into medicine and heavenly rosewater. (Like the Japanese maple, I'm happy to say that the so-named "damask" rose helpfully reveals its provenance in Damascus, Syria.) From here the love affair with all things roses makes its way across the Persian plateau, along the Hindu Kush and straight to the topographical heart of the Indian subcontinent. The scent, like the flower, is then transported to Moorish Spain and farther west, conveyed as an object of shared fascination and a symbol of cross-pollination between the Islamic and Christian worlds.

I have it on good authority that the hybrid tea rose, the mother of all English roses, bears a complex lineage of earlier hybrids including *Rosa moschata* (aka autumn damask), as well as *Rosa phoenicia* and *Rosa gallica* (aka summer damask). As Allen Paterson attests, in his beautifully illustrated *The History of the Rose*, some of these rose ancestors likely arrived in western Europe with the advance of Islam, at its zenith during Europe's medieval period.[6] But, according to Paterson, it was the *Rosa chinensis* (aka Slater's crimson China) that travelled from China to western Europe in the late eighteenth century, where it became the subject of much horticultural tinkering, and gave birth to its occidental offspring, the hybrid tea. If the hybrid tea is the mother of all English roses, I like to think of *Rosa chinensis* as its natural grandmother. When one starts to really dig into the horticultural supply chain the chances of finding one's way back to China, a region that holds one-eighth of the world's total plant species, are as great as that formidable wall. I recently discovered that even the Japanese anemone, a plant whose common name ostensibly identifies its point of origin, was first found or cultivated in China. And yet, while I can name at least a dozen or more English rose cultivars, including Slater's crimson China, I can't come up with so much as the generic name for the rose in Mandarin.

Even though all this talk of hybridization paints a seemingly rosy picture of cross-cultural influence between East and West, we might turn to another rose variety before we jump to such optimistic conclusions: namely, the apothecary rose. The history of this rose might tell a different story – that plants, like people, have not always travelled as ambassadors of friendship and mutually enriching exchanges. For legend has it the apothecary rose (so named because nineteenth-century French pharmacists grew this specimen in pots outside their shop entrances), travelled to western Europe in medieval times by way of other channels. Hardly a symbol of peace (an alternate name for one variety of hybrid tea rose is the peace rose), the apothecary rose was purportedly championed as a spoil of war, a memento for Christian Crusaders determined to capture the Holy Lands from the alleged infidels. Whether this piece of

By Any Other Name

chivalric lore be false or true, the rose assumed, by the thirteenth century, its heraldic profile in the royal English courts, recorded by a monk at St. Mary's Abbey as "ye badge of England and hath growne in that countrye for as long as ye mynde of man goeth."[7]

I, too, can attest to the dogged persistence of the rose in my own childhood English garden, when my family lived in Britain from 1975 to 1981. My father was no stranger to epic migrations as the son of a merchant-family from Mumbai who made the great exodus, during Partition, from a newly created India to a newly created Pakistan. He was a child at the time – one of those "midnight's children" born around the time of each nation's birth at the stroke of midnight, on August 14, 1947. The Pirbhai family had made a name for themselves in the cotton-processing industry and, by the 1970s, my father expanded into the car industry; the family might have enjoyed considerable political and financial clout had they stayed in Pakistan. But these were the volatile decades of a fledgling state ruled by those who could make or unmake family fortunes with the stroke of a pen, or something much sharper, and I guess my father was willing to lose in status what he hoped to gain, in the West, in security and peace of mind. So we – my parents, my older brother and I – moved to England, along with my grandmother, one of my uncles and a set of aunts and cousins. Unfortunately, family grievances and fractures, the kind that soap operas are made of, complete with brotherly rivalries, sibling resentments, maternal favouritism, split allegiances, deceased patriarchs and inheritance disputes, cast a longer shadow over our household than any corrupt politician ever could.

For now, I'd rather don my own rose-coloured glasses and

focus on more peaceable times in our then newly adopted land. A few years after our arrival, we moved into a new home in a town called Sunningdale, in Berkshire county, some fifty kilometres west of London. Moving out of the financial and increasingly multiethnic capital, where opportunities abounded for enterprising immigrants, seemed like a risky business, and I'm still not clear what precipitated this move, like so many of our moves to come. I can only offer three possible explanations, in descending order of creative speculation. The first, a romantic one: my father wanted to get us out of a congested, crime-ridden city, buy a home with real English bones, enrol his kids in posh English schools where they could learn to speak like *the upstairs* people, put down roots, live the dream. The second, an armchair psychologist's explanation: the more antagonized the relationship between my father and his family became, the greater his tendency to upend his own family and make impulsive moves and migrations, as if physical distance was the only way he knew how to extricate himself from those emotional triggers. And the last and most fanciful explanation: the children who were thrown into the great human chain of migration during the earth-shattering Partition years had developed a curious affliction – namely, the inability to stand still long enough to locate "home" in the new lands they came to occupy. (Not so fanciful if one considers the millions of diasporic South Asians living anywhere *but* the Indian subcontinent.)

Whatever the reason, our first true English home brought with it a stiff, formal garden, lacking any of the cottagey charm I now associate with English country gardens. A lone walnut tree stood at the centre of the front lawn, calling attention to its, and perhaps our (the only brown family for miles around this 1970s English idyll), difference. The two cherry trees off to one side were a nice touch but only produced the most unpalatable bitter fruit (strange that

By Any Other Name

my mother is now buried under a cherry tree, likely as inedible, in Montreal). But there was one aspect to this garden that was full-on English: a substantial rose bed off to one side. Curiously, this island bed was shaped like a crescent moon, as if in anticipation of the Muslim family who would one day come to tend it. The previous homeowner, much like our own predecessor here in Waterloo, had put much effort and love into those rose cultivars, giving them a position of pride; we knew this because it was the only herbaceous bed set away from the perimeter and well into the garden proper.

One day, some six months after my sister, Nooreen, was born, the first truly joyous memory created in that house, a photographer dropped by. I'm not sure if he was a professional photographer or an acquaintance with an expensive camera but someone, other than my parents, was taking pictures that day. Since the sun beamed down on the cloud-covered land, we were corralled into the garden for a family portrait, despite Mum's protest that she was ill-prepared for such exhibitionism, makeup-less, hair unkempt and in an outfit reserved for a day of sundry household duties. *Woman, thou doth protest too much* must have been whispered into her ear and she reconciled herself to the impromptu family portrait. In a one-acre garden that offered both a sunny and shady countenance, the question arose: On which side should we stand? Mum was quick to suggest the shady side where we had more trees. *That would make a nice backdrop*, I remember her saying. If I had any say in the matter I would have agreed, because that's the side where I played hide-and-seek with my schoolmates; the side where two trees served as goalposts for football tosses with my brother; the side with a garden gate providing access to the outside world, like a portal to a little girl's land of make-believe. But Camera Fellow favoured the other side, the sunny side – the side where the roses grew. Mum put a hand to her forehead, saying she had woken up with a migraine, hoping at least one of the men would show some sensitivity to her photosensitivity. And even though she loved her garden, she had never much cared for the roses, always complaining about the thorns and the amount of fussing and tending they needed. *And for what?* I can just hear her now because I've since inherited the migraines and an antipathy for roses. *They look nice enough in flower but without those blossoms they're just scrappy-looking shrubs.* But poor Mum was as outranked as her kids, and we fell into an awkwardly strained huddle in front of the crescent-shaped rose bed.

As it turned out, the side of the garden where the roses grew was the side from which most of the pictures of this Sunningdale house were taken. At least the ones that haven't been lost to our subsequent moves or overexposed, like we were that day, to a stranger's gaze. One of these pictures has captured the back of the house, everything behind it in a veil of mist. I can just barely see the pink drapes in my second-storey bedroom window, with a climbing rose of some sort right below it. Off to the far left is a wall of shrubs and trees, some ours and some part of the borrowed landscape, its edges lost to that mist-covered morning. And right in the foreground is one-half of that half-moon crescent. Generous heads of red and pastel yellow balance precariously atop twiggy branches that do, as Mum described, look rather scrappy, at least when denuded of flower. Someone is standing behind this bed of roses, taking the picture. Someone has taken care to place the

rose bed in the foreground, as if it is the real object of interest. The roses leer at us but at least in this picture, unlike in the family portrait, we have a view of the house, as Mum wanted, and a view of that other side, where the grass was always greener and the trees provided shade. The side where I spent at least a few childhood years frolicking with the neighbours' kids, singing "Ring-a-ring o' roses / A pocket full of posies." Before the storybook ending of a proper English life in a proper English garden was foreclosed on us, and it *all fell down*.

The English rose, for all its noble lineage and familial memories of English country homes, does not suffuse me with nostalgia. And as much as the roses in our Sunningdale home conjure up a history of routes, we were supplanted far too quickly and too suddenly for roots to ever run deep there.

So I turn to another rose: the South Asian rose. Gul.

The Urdu word is borrowed directly from the Farsi word *gul* for *rose*, itself a telling signifier of the rich cultural, linguistic and botanical gifts shared between Persian and Mughal civilizations. It was gul, this heavily scented, multi-petalled flower, that sent poets into states of rapture and emperors into fits of passion. In Sufi poet Hafiz's imaginary gardens, gul perfumes the air we breathe, a metonym for heavenly scents, or nothing less than the *heaven-sent*. And pushing at the conventions of his time, where the sacred and profane mesh in wine-guzzling tropes, Hafiz advises, "Friends: better to tend to pleasure while the rose blossoms / it's the world of the lover and we'll drink with pleasure."[8] Mughal wordsmiths were no less spellbound by *gul*, never to be outdone by their Persian influencers. One of the most beloved Urdu-language poets, Mirza

Ghalib, looks to the rose as muse for the ghazal, his poetic couplet of choice: "This blooming red rose / is sired by the spring / and gives tongue to my lucid eloquence."[9] And as if poetry does not a crafty love letter make to this universally lauded flower, the first Mughal emperor, Babur, a poet in his own right, went so far as to name his daughters Gulrang (Rose-Coloured), GulChihra (Rose-Cheeked) and Gulbadan (Rose-Body).

I imagine even many a stalwart colonial, like my own great-grandfather, a district commissioner from Wales stationed in the dusty outposts of the British Raj, were hard-pressed to turn up their distinctly Anglo-Saxon noses at the fragrances wafting from Mughal gardens and Rajput palaces. Though you'd think British colonial chroniclers would have noted, as did an earlier traveller by the name of Abdur Razzaq, a Muslim diplomat from Persia who visited the royal Mughal palaces several centuries earlier, that "these people [of India] could not live without roses and they look upon these as quite as necessary as food."[10] And Abdur Razzaq was not speaking in tongues. In the Indian subcontinent, people don't just plant roses for their horticultural beauty – they eat them!

If you've ever been to an Indian restaurant anywhere from Tottenham to Toronto, and ordered that most common of dessert menu items, the gulab jamun, you might be surprised to learn that the dish is named for its rosewater-infused syrup. We also consume gulkand, a preserve made with rose petals, for its healing properties, and many a South Asian mouth is stained red from the habitual chewing of paan, a betel-leaf slathered with katha, a red paste derived from the khair tree (or acacia), which is notably sweetened by a dollop of this saccharine gulkand. We drink sharbat and Rooh Afza, cordials made from rose essence, mostly for their refreshing palate, but also during Ramazan when they are ritualistically consumed at the end of a day's fast. We sprinkle rosewater on the savoury (biryanis and yoghurt-based kormas) as much as the sweet (rice-based desserts such as phirni and khir). While parents across North America resort to pouring chocolate syrup into milk to make it more palatable to kids, South Asian parents serve up Pepto Bismol–pink concoctions of milk drenched in rose syrup. And Pakistani kids are often found flocking street-food vendors, where gastronomical maestros serve up one of the nation's most popular "edible" drinks: the faluda, which is part milkshake and part dessert, made up of sweet basil seeds, vermicelli noodles, milk, ice cream and that most important of all ingredients, rose syrup.

But in the rose-lexicon of sensory triggers, the non-edible attar (the signature rose-scented perfume of the Islamic world) takes the cake. We now know that our sense of smell is the first to develop – a fetus is able to smell its amniotic world by its sixth month in the womb. And it is the dominant sense till preadolescence, which is why the smells emanating from our parents' or guardians' kitchens can take us right back to our infancy. Maybe this is why the spiritual and cultural currency of the rose can no more be extricated from my olfactory senses than a rose-addled metaphor from a Sufi poet's oration. Interestingly, attar takes me back to family as much as to place. One whiff and I am eight years old again, sitting cross-legged on a botanically inspired Isfahan rug, now cleared of furniture for a circle of mourners, in my grandmother's living room in a London

Garden Inventories

flat. My grandmother is holding a prayer-service for my uncle, who died of a heart attack in his late forties, one less knot binding the warp and weft of the Pirbhai clan.

My fidgety childish brain can't prevent itself from sneaking peeks at this largely adult group. Their heads are bowed as their fingers nimbly count off a string of black tasbi beads (rosaries) for each completion of the Surah al-Fatiha, the Quranic "opening" prayer. These are the prayers that I will come to recite, three and four decades hence, as gul-scented incense sticks burn down to embers at my mother's and father's freshly dug graves in Quebec and Ontario respectively. As I survey the room, I land on my grandmother's stern gaze, and I bow my head in mortified obedience to a woman whose countenance seemed frozen in a singular expression of disapproval. Generated by some perverse combination of religious zeal, the stigma of widowhood and matriarchal tyranny, one such disapproving look could induce a trifecta of fear, guilt and shame bonded together like a wrecking ball of internalized terror. In fact, I think she terrified me then as much as I realize she must have terrified my father, even in the ensuing decades of their estrangement.

Though surely it was my eldest aunt who paid the heftiest price as the first-born daughter to this long-suffering widowed matriarch, for it was her special lot in life to forfeit her own life (a husband and family of her own, that sort of thing) and play servant-maiden to her mother till the latter's dying breath. Even now my grandmother appears to have dominated my attention and I have lost sight of my poor aunt making her way around that circle of mourners. Too scared to bring my head up again, I roll my eyeballs to the top of my head and get a peripheral view of my aunt making her way around the circle. Her arthritic knees snap, crackle and pop like my favourite cereal as she stoops before each bowed head. I detect a mourner's arm extending like a cuckoo clock bird at the strike of

By Any Other Name

an hour, just far enough for my aunt to dab a wrist with a droplet released from a miniature glass bottle. The arm retreats back to the mourner's lap, and so the ritual continues till a shadow looms over me. My brother nudges me to extend my arm and I sense a fragrant raindrop landing on my wrist. I snatch a quick look at my aunt making her way to an empty spot in the circle, dutifully stationed by her mother's side, where she and her explosive joints steal a moment's repose. And then the miniature bottle is withdrawn from the folds of a billowing sari and placed on the floral-patterned border of my grandmother's rug. The circle is complete. Attar suffuses the room, and faces emerge from the shadow of black dupattas and skullcap kufis as noses tingle, suddenly alive to this welcome change in the quality of air. I think there must be some genie-like magic in a bottle so small but powerful enough to turn a room suffocating with latent hostilities, sadness and grief into a garden of roses. Not the kind awaiting us in our Sunningdale home, but the kind lost in the homeland left behind – the kind this circle of adults would be mourning, in perpetuity.

So far from these homelands, we, too, forget the names of things and *gul* is once again lost to the supremacy of the *rose*, a shrubby flowering plant that has turned the Canadian landscape into a quintessentially English garden, steeped in legends, myths and folklore as old as medieval Europe and as mystical as Venus, the Roman love goddess herself. For isn't the rose, in its truest form, also the flower of Venus, its five-petals corresponding to the five points of the star? Perhaps this is why roses rain down on Venus's birth in Botticelli's ethereal painting. But once again I am getting sucked into the vortex of other traditions – so much so that I am forgetting that roses belong not only to the cultural and mythological landscapes of Europe and Asia but also to North America, which has several of its own native varieties. One variety is the rudely named swamp rose (one of those early colonial settler names collected in Catharine Parr Traill's flora, perhaps).

The swamp rose is arguably an apt descriptor for a shrub that resides in some rather boggy places, like the marshy marginalia of the Great Lakes or the windswept coastal banks of the North Atlantic. But contrary to its name, the native rose possesses a scent far sweeter than any commercial variety I've come across in local nurseries. In Ontario, among the Anishinaabeg, the native rose also possesses a much sweeter name: *oginiig*. And as the rose has already shown us, every name has a story. I am truly thankful for the story of *oginiig*, which I am paraphrasing here from a number of sources, careful not to appropriate any single telling, and in the awareness

that all such "creation stories are sacred to the people who hold them."[11] Also, it is important to note that, in this case, *rose* is used as a translation of *oginiig*.

The story of *oginiig* goes something like this: Roses were so common on Turtle Island that no one noticed when their numbers started to decrease, along with their variety and range. Only Hummingbird, Bee and Bear knew something was wrong, as the honey yields were depleted and less appetizing. Each one blamed the other until one summer the roses were no more. This was called the Summer of the Disappearance of the Rose. It was alarming enough for a grand meeting to be called, where everyone discussed what could be done to rectify this appalling situation. No one had a solution till one day Hummingbird travelled to a far-off land and found a rather sickly, solitary rose on a mountainside, which he carried home to the medicine men and women. When Rose was healed and brought back to life, she was able to give witness to her family's destruction. *It was the rabbits!* she said to an outraged audience, including Bear who set off to punish these greedy rabbits. But Rose interceded, saying the rabbits were not to shoulder all the blame for the roses' demise, as they had only taken advantage of the fact that no one else had shown any concern for her kind at their time of need. Rose's argument was as fair as it was sound, and the rabbits were released, though not without a scar to remind everyone of their bad behaviour. Then the rose was given thorns to protect it from the kind of greedy appetites the rabbits had displayed, and to caution others from taking for granted the delicate balance between plants, humans and animals. They were one family, after all, and to neglect any one member was to neglect them all.

Like *oginiig*, the Anishinaabeg word for *rose*, Métis artist Christi Belcourt's paintings convey a different picture, tell a sweeter story. Born in Scarborough, Ontario, but from the mânitow sâkahikan Métis community in Lac Ste. Anne, Alberta, Belcourt describes the floral beadwork principles and patterns found in her artwork as "one of the most central artistic legacies Métis grandmothers have left to us."[12] I had the privilege of viewing a few of Belcourt's monumental paintings while they were exhibited at Wilfrid Laurier University's Robert Langen Art Gallery, in Fall 2022, a time during which I was ruminating on all things roses for this book. And there she was: Belcourt's stylized representation of the native rose. This rose reappears, like other native flora, in many of Belcourt's paintings, including *Water Song*,[13] where wild roses dance freely among trilliums, blueberries, plantains, strawberries, yarrows, thistles, chokecherries, burdocks, milkweeds and other native flora. This is no rose of the swamps. This is a rose to be celebrated in songs of diversity, interrelation and continuity. This rose is a thing of beauty, its open-faced five-petalled head held high, its foliage outstretched, like open hands, in a prayer of gratitude, to these grandmothers, perhaps – the kind who teach their children's children how to create gardens out of glass beads. The kind that little girl on a floral-patterned rug in a London flat would have longed for. The kind she still longs for.

How can a name like *rose* not be perceived as beautiful when it is an anagram for *Eros*. For love itself. We love the rose as much as we love to wax poetic about love in the name of the rose. But the rose, as a cultural and linguistic signifier, alerts me to the gaps in my own knowledge, like the potential errors in transmission of our botanical recordkeeping. Names can and do tell an important story about the way plants, like people, travel. But sometimes the stories they tell are pure fiction – perhaps like the myth of origin itself. And maybe that is the trouble with all these English and Latin names in the Canadian context – they are cultural constructs that, much of the time, also tell stories of wilful erasure. A genocide of names.

Browsing through a list of award-winning British and American roses in the type of catalogue from which I imagine Don once selected specimens for his aspirational rose garden, I am struck by the dazzling range of personages as well as the sheer artistry of

By Any Other Name

names attributed to the rose: *Beautiful Britain, Penny Lane, Grand Masterpiece, Queen Elizabeth, Chrysler Imperial, Mountbatten, President's Choice, American Beauty.* But as I work my way through this list, I am equally struck by how so many of these names tell stories of other places, and other histories. Stories of *elsewhere*. And I struggle to find stories of here.

As a nation of immigrants, settlers and Indigenous peoples whose communities are as diverse as the plants stored in our individual and collective memory banks, we might well expect the names for these plants will sprout stories of elsewhere. And like the sun to chlorophyll, these stories are a vital ingredient in the Story of Us. But each one, on its own, is that sickly, withering flower. It is a father holding on to grievances buried so deep that he can't stop and smell the roses standing right in front of him. It is a war of ascension. Of whose story matters more. Of who gets to have their place in the sun, like those empires on which the sun never sets. It is not the whole story. It is not Eros.

With *rose*, we see only one side to the story. With *gul*, we see another. With *oginiig*, we see ever deeper. And then another story appears, out of this mist of names: *méiguī*.

玫瑰

Anthropology of the Cottage, or a (Second?) Slice of Precambrian Pie

Pandemics and Staycations

It was COVID times, one year into quarantine, a second summer season on the horizon without the prospect of travel, at least until Doug Ford's Conservative government lifted the non-essential travel ban in Ontario. A collective sigh of relief reverberated across the province's one million square kilometres. Ford may as well have declared world peace. After all, this meant that people were free to do that most human of things: to wander, to roam, to venture outside their proverbial backyards. But where would they go, still province-bound as they were? Was there anywhere to go? Most hotels and other public facilities, including campsites and provincial parks, were restricted to limited capacities, if they were open at all. And yet, our neighbourhood in southwestern Ontario emptied out almost as fast as Ford could hop into his own pickup truck.

One could safely bet the provincial leader was heading "up north" to a place Ontarians refer to as "cottage country." Cottage country is not simply a destination. Cottage country is a sacred place. Going there is a kind of pilgrimage. In fact, some months earlier, Ford had come under fire for driving to this recreational mecca, seemingly tone-deaf to local mayors begging the government to keep the urbanites away from their rural hamlets. When asked why he would violate his own public health measures, Ford contritely told reporters he had made the briefest of trips to the "family cottage" to check on the plumbing.[1] I am sure many of my neighbours could relate to Ford's compulsion to risk public censure for the sake of cottage upkeep. After all, they have cottages, too. And anyone who lives in Canada knows that water expands when it freezes, and sometimes even shutting off the water, which I imagine most cottage owners must do before the winter months, doesn't prevent pipes from bursting. If Ford had some tinkering to do up there in his family cottage, he was in good company.

But when the travel restriction ban was lifted, some cottage-*less* folks, like Ronaldo and I, were at a loss. For us, mobility did not involve northward excursions to the Canadian wilderness, and "movement," be it personal or professional, usually assumed a more transcontinental reach involving passports, customs, security gates and air travel. A staycation, for us, was a literal affair: with nowhere in the world or the nation on which to set our sights, we were home to stay. While thousands crammed their SUVs with groceries and household items for their annual cottage excursions to the various

Anthropology of the Cottage

and sundry woodsy hideaways dotting the province's 250,000 lakes, including the Great Lakes of Ontario, Huron, Superior and Erie, we were home to watch the exodus unfold. We were home to witness the emptying out of our streets and, with it, the evacuated sounds of suburban summer, like children thrashing about in swimming pools and the lawn-mower opera. We were left to parlay with the ghosts of summers passed.

All that stillness and quietude made me wonder what manner of alchemy this cottage country must possess that a political leader would risk his own populist hide or turn a suburban street like ours into a virtual ghost town. Could this "up north" destination hold the same kind of promise that the proverbial *el norte* – that is, North America minus Mexico – held for so many of us, the new or recent immigrants who arrived here, sometimes at great risk and expense, from the lands of the equatorial south? I could only conclude that "up north" was, indeed, another kind of mecca; a land of milk and honey. And maybe this was the year, with nowhere else to go and province-bound as we were, to strap on our own GPS trackers and follow the exodus into that other promised land, even farther north than the *el norte* of our own mythological mappings.

> ***An Earthly Paradise: Lakefront Cottage***
> *The Cottage takes you back in time, a time of simplicity and pre-internet fun! Get ready to enjoy the entire property and cottage, but please review pics and descriptions to determine if this cottage and property is suitable for your vacation. A true earthly paradise.*
>
> ***RE: Inquiry at Earthly Paradise***
> *From: Mariam Pirbhai*
> *Re: inquiry for june cottage rental*

Hello,
I would like to know your rate and availability for a cottage (occupancy: 2) for mid- to end-June, 2021. Do you have television or wifi? And is this part of a larger resort, or an independent cottage?
Thanks,
Mariam

Marian,
We have openings for that week. Our weekly rate for a 2 bedroom cottage is $1695 – plus HST. We have 12 independent cottages. We do not have TVs but do have wifi in all cottages. Thanks for your interest.
Helen

Here: Cottage! There: Hut!

I was born in Karachi, Pakistan, the country's most densely populated city in its southernmost region of Sindh. And I came to live in England, the Philippines and, for a very brief period, the United Arab Emirates, before my family immigrated to Canada in the late 1980s. All of the above countries are notably coastal. Even in Canada, our port of entry was in Halifax, Nova Scotia, as if my father was saying, "See, we're not so very different from those other million or so Europeans who once looked for safe harbour at Canadian ports." Of course, my father had no knowledge of Pier 21 at the time; we got here on a one-way economy airfare, via a circuitous route that included stopovers in the United States (a far cry from the Continuous Journey regulation that Prime Minister Wilfrid Laurier legislated in 1908, as the only legal means of entry into Canada for hopeful migrants, though Tamil refugees on board the M.V. *Sun Sea*, turned away on account of this very same law a century later, might beg to differ). However, we were

Anthropology of the Cottage

hardly refugees, arriving on an entrepreneurial visa (i.e., business immigration for the self-employed), and I have little experience of boats, big or small. Still, arriving at Canada's historic port city seems befitting for people born on the distant shores of another coastline: the Arabian Sea.

I only bring up these coastal happenstances because my concept of a holiday or summer home is likewise associated with beach dunes and salt water. In Pakistan these coastal homes did not come in the form of wood-panelled cabins much less magazine-worthy Shangri-La's; these were rather makeshift concrete constructions erected along the shorelines of the Arabian Sea. These beach homes, at least the few I remember from my very brief childhood in, and ever more ephemeral return trips to, Pakistan, were designed for sporadic afternoon getaways from the city in places called Sandspit or Hawke's Bay. I have a picture (likely taken in the late 1960s) of my mother (seen here in blue pants and shirt, kneeling in the centre of a group) at one of these beach excursions, a glimpse of one of the larger sets of "huts"  visible in the background. For us children, these seaside getaways entailed some kind of chaperone in the form of one's elders playing interminable rounds of cards – rummy, poker, flush were games of choice – while we lobbed cricket balls into the sea or took camel rides along the beach. For the unmarried, these seaside shacks were far enough from Karachi's city centre to be earmarked for romantic trysts or any type of social gathering unfettered by the pious gaze of those same elders and, in multigenerational family homes, the even more pious elders' elders. Though the waters are shallow and calm from October to March, swimming was not top of mind; card-playing washed down with contraband whisky (Pakistan is an Islamic Republic) held greater appeal, at least to the rabble-rousing jet set that was my parents' entourage. But the beach homes lining Sandspit, at least those in the rear-view mirror of my childhood memories, were utilitarian places, set up with the barest amenities, even though for many in that city of fourteen million it was far more "house" than anyone could afford. However, as is the way with privilege – it's safe to say that anyone with a supplemental property reserved strictly for leisure falls on the side of *the haves* – these homes were considered somewhat superfluous and rudimentary. They were not even regarded as homes. They were more typically referred to as "huts." Huts with basic toiletry: a bucket, a faucet, a sink. Huts with some sort of cooking facility and a "cot" or two in the event someone needed an afternoon siesta or craved something a bit, shall we say, spicier than chicken sandwiches and Johnnie Walker.

Perhaps since the 1970s of my childhood, these beach huts have morphed into something you might see on a *House Hunters International* episode – the kind focused on sunny destinations where wealthy financiers relinquish the rat race for early retirement in tax havens like Panama and Turks and Caicos. Perhaps millennial Pakistanis have turned to flipping the family beach hut into revenue-generating properties, renting them out to intrepid tourists with all the frills and thrills of an Airbnb listing. It is possible that my childhood recollections are mistaken – I was five years old when we emigrated – and these beach huts were never quite as rudimentary as I remember them. I also don't wish to perpetuate any stereotypes of "Third World" backwardness. God knows, Muslim

Anthropology of the Cottage

societies have enough bad orientalist press to deal with. Come to think of it, perhaps those holiday constructions were referred to as "huts" precisely because they were never intended to be occupied for any length of time. Perhaps their rudimentariness was, much like rustic cabins in the woods, a part of the allure. Maybe Pakistanis are equally enchanted by the idea of roughing it, after all, if we have the audacity to refer to any sort of recreational pastime as a form of "roughing it" in a country where the majority of the population subsists on the equivalent of a few hundred (US) dollars per month. The likelier explanation might be that the beach hut was a mere diversion for those whose actual holidays were reserved for longer excursions abroad, be it for leisure or, more likely, for the purpose of visiting relatives (the South Asian diaspora is the largest in the world and chances are that every family *inside* their homeland has some family *outside* their homeland).

When I first heard the term *cottage* bandied about in Ontario, I imagined the beach huts of my childhood. I pictured short weekend getaways, spicy dalliances, romantic trysts, contraband booze (it seems so much more interesting than a pit stop at the Liquor Control Board of Ontario), cricket bats, camel rides and chicken sandwiches. What I had not imagined was the amount of time spent *thinking about* and the amount of time spent *in* these cottages. The amount of thought and preparation given to cottage life. The weeks and months spent at the cottage, at the exclusion of all other travel. The amount of family history and heritage bound up in these cottages. The amount of scrimping and saving or inheritance windfall spending to make the cottage dream a reality. Did I already mention the amount of time spent in these cottages? Entire summers. Summer upon summer. A lifetime of summers. Sometimes even autumnal weekends. Sometimes, for the more adventurous, winter getaways. And for a smaller minority, a retirement

Garden Inventories

destination. Adding up the time, the cost, the history, the heritage, the memories, one might even say these cottages are treated as second homes. Indeed, they are homes, with plumbing, electricity and central heating, with well-stocked kitchens and linen closets, with decorative memorabilia and furnished porches. Homes that may be shuttered and unused in the depths of winter, but homes nonetheless.

There: beach hut. Temporary. Built on sand and therefore shifting, unstable. A here today, gone tomorrow kind of space. Purely recreational. A matter of privilege but hardly of the aspirational sort. (If you asked me whether my family had, at any point, owned one of these beach huts I would not be able to confirm or deny such hut-ownership.) Most definitely *not* a home.

Here: cottage. Enduring. Patrimony. Built on the Canadian Shield. A place to be fussed over. Loved. An object of reverence and aspiration. (If you ask a neighbour if they own a cottage, denial would only be proffered by those not wishing to disclose financial capital, in much the same way it is deemed impolite to ask fellow Canadians about their political leanings or where they come from.) Most definitely a home, or a home away from home.

> ***Sunset Cove Cottages***
> *Our location is second to none, on a quiet cove with a safe beach for children, a fire pit for shore dinners and evening bonfires, and spectacular sunsets. We're also close to golf courses, nature trails and quiet country roads for cycling.*
>
> ***RE: Inquiry at Sunset Cove Cottages***
> *From: Mariam*
> *Subject: availability/rate*

Anthropology of the Cottage

Hello,
We would like to know your rate and availability for mid-June to end June (occupancy: 2). We are looking for some privacy rather than a large family resort.
Thanks,
Mariam

Hi Miriam
Thanks for thinking of us and yes, we are a small resort (three cottages), very quiet and peaceful. Our cottages include bed linens, fully equipped kitchen, BBQ (and propane) and we also have a canoe and bicycles for camp use. The fire pit is for your use and as much wood as you like is free. And did we mention that we have NO mozzies or black flies at any time? Trust this meets your requirements!
Earl

Keeping Up with the Joneses

Summer vacation home. Holiday home. Cabin in the woods. Roughing it in the bush. None of these are quintessentially Canadian ideas in their own right, but they are part of a distinctly Canadian mythology that is both as highly localized as it is broadly nationalist. Cottage season, for those alien to Canadian weather and how militantly it governs our lives, appears to have the royal blessing, starting with a long weekend to commemorate Queen Victoria's birthday in the latter half of May, and ending around Canadian Thanksgiving in mid-October. Once we toss in the word *cottage*, be it as a noun such as the *family cottage*, a verb such as *cottaging* or even an adjective such as *cottage life*, the picture narrows even further, and one might conjure images of children diving into black-bottomed lakes, grown-ups lounging on Adirondack chairs as they sip Coors Light or Niagara-harvested wines, happy

Garden Inventories

families conversing around an evening firepit under eerie shadows of spruce, pine and sumac. Throw proper nouns like *Georgian Bay*, *the Muskokas* or *the Kawarthas* into this idyllic cocktail and we start getting at something that is not only uniquely Canadian, but uniquely Ontarian.

I watch neighbours engage in the ritual of cottage preparation. My neighbours mainly consist of Ontario's upper middle class of skilled professionals, and many are of German or Scottish ancestry, as is characteristic of the old settlements in the city of Waterloo. They are good folk. They come to each other's aid during snowstorms. They alert each other to any untoward activity, like break-ins, car thefts and even coyote sightings, all of which are, thankfully, quite rare. When called upon they always provide helpful recommendations to local tradespeople, like plumbers, contractors and electricians. And collectively they form a pleasant community that will never shortchange you a smile or a wave at a polite but, more often than not, conservative arm's-length.

Some neighbours are not cottage owners but they are annual cottage-*goers*. Where exactly they go, and to whose cottage, remains a mystery, but I know that this is where they go because, in their taciturn way, they tell me so. That is, now that I have been schooled in the shorthand language relating to cottage life, I know what and where *up north*, *long weekend traffic*, *downtime*, *decompress* and *spot of fishing* consists of. Even without such a smorgasbord of verbal clues, the motorized fishing boats parked alongside pickup trucks and SUVs in suburban driveways are a dead giveaway. Lengthy stretches of time can be spent in these stationary boats during the spring and summer months. The responsible boat owner knows that these are mechanical objects that can do serious harm if not maintained, but some of this upkeep is of the cosmetic kind: vacuuming interiors, polishing chrome bits and bobs, and hosing

Anthropology of the Cottage

down fibreglass exteriors. Such tinkering can go on for weeks before neighbours take off in a caravan of pickup trucks all souped up to cart speedboats to their natural habitat: the opaque surfaces of glacial lakes.

Of course, when I hear neighbours telling neighbours, "I'll be up at the lake," I have learned to take navigational terms like *up* and articles like *the* with a grain of salt. *Up* could be down, at the southerly shores of the Great Lakes of Ontario and Erie; it could take you southwest to the sand dunes of Lake Huron, or northwest, to the inlets of Georgian Bay; and yes, it could certainly be north – far, far, far up north, to the perimeters of Lake Superior or, to the most adventurous, as far as Pickle Lake, Ontario's northernmost point by car (a whopping two thousand kilometres from Waterloo). It could also take you to the province's interior, where lakes, big and small, are as numerous as the cars fleeing the city on a long weekend. In a province characterized by, and one might even say built around, this distinctive water feature (a whopping 55 percent of Ontarians live in and around the Golden Horseshoe, or the northwestern perimeter of Lake Ontario), "the lake" is itself a floating signifier. The province even takes its name from the lake, rather than the other way around. *Ontario* is drawn from the Mohawk word *Kaniatari:io*, which translates as "nice or beautiful lake."[2] Though here, and anywhere Indigenous names are used in this book, I defer to Daniel Coleman's cautionary reminder that Indigenous languages, like Indigenous stories, have been so long filtered through the muddied waters of the English language and the colonial psyche, that all such translations are as "contested and shifting" as our attempts to contain them. Coleman nonetheless agrees that "the longhouse people must have thought the lake enchanting to give it such a name."[3] Indeed, if you've ever flown across the province at a lower elevation, as I once did on a domestic flight from Toronto to Montreal, you'd have been awestruck by the immensity of Lake Ontario as well as the sheer number of smaller (but by no means small) lakes covering the province. When you're looking down on these patches of blue as they catch the sun's glare, they shimmer and sparkle like mega-pop-star Rihanna's diamonds. Lakes and rivers make up one-fifth of the province's area but lakes reign supreme here.

These summer excursions are not unusual in their own right. It is when cottage excursions come at the expense of all other forms of travel that the armchair anthropologist in me kicks in: If a travel itinerary involves repetition, sameness and familiarity at the exclusion of most other forms and destinations of travel, what might such single-mindedness say about this kind of traveller? I turn to a trained anthropologist for an answer. Julia Harrison's *A Timeless Place: The Ontario Cottage* stands out as the most in-depth study of this "rather curious" (her words, not mine!) local phenomenon. Like me, Harrison settled in Ontario later in life, and soon started noticing the mental, physical, financial and even political tenor of cottage culture. For Harrison, much of this was distilled through a set of value judgments and assumptions that "[she] would be going to [her] cottage at every opportunity, or negotiating as much time as [she] could at a relative's or friend's cottage, or failing these two options, [she] would spend [her] summer lamenting the sad reality that [she] was not at a cottage on the shores of a nearby lake."[4] In other words, Harrison detected that there is something unique about the way Ontarians, at least a segment of the population, spend their summers and, perhaps more significantly, mythologize cottage ownership as central to that experience.

Harrison's informative book reminds me not to paint all cottagers with the same brush. All cottagers, like cottage regions, are not made equal. Some are more affluent than others. Some more

Anthropology of the Cottage

ostentatious than others. Some more community-minded than others. Some are what she terms "traditionalists" who view cottage country as the simpler way, uncluttered by the trappings of consumerism and modernity – the cabin-in-the-woods types whose great-grandfathers may have been among the postwar generation who were either given land outright or bought it for rock-bottom prices from a government parcelling it out like Halloween candy, building their humble cabins from the ground up, pinewood plank by pinewood plank. Some are "socialites" who see the cottage as an extension of their wealth and flaunt it as such, bringing many of the conveniences and trappings of consumer-driven culture with them. And some are what she calls the "transients" – the renters or time-share holders. There are transients who exhibit some of the values and attitudes of traditionalists, having "long-standing relationships with particular cottages, lakes, and communities." So even here, among the transients, there is a degree of repetition, return and connection. One might imagine that many of these transients aspire to become permanent cottage owners, or at least sow the seed of cottage ownership in their offspring who have grown up sharing in this family tradition.

Ah, tradition. The stuff that cultural dreams are made of. As Harrison notes, cottages and tradition are synonymous here, as this is where the sacredness of memory is moulded and nurtured. At least for some. Really, just a minority. Because some traditions, it would seem, are costly. So perhaps this is a good moment to get into some of the more pecuniary aspects of cottage experience. I must confess to my own sticker shock when we started looking into the possibility of a cottage rental last summer during Ford's sanctioned staycation. On average, a week's stay starts at around $1,500, and continues to rise at alarming rates, based on desirability of location, waterfront versus non-waterfront, property size, dock access,

Garden Inventories

amenities like Wi-Fi or satellite television, independent cottages in private settings versus cottages in resorts, and the list goes on. I also considered the amount of gas required to travel between home and cottage over great distances, since public transport to the so-called hinterland is almost impossible to come by. As for commutes, the average trip to cottage country can involve a minimum two-hour drive from Waterloo (about the same from Toronto), and very often amounts to four plus hours if one is heading farther north to the Muskokas or Kawarthas. Conclusion: upward mobility is a literal and figurative requirement for cottage life. And for those regular cottage-goers, other associated costs such as boats, boat maintenance, cottage (aka house) maintenance (think Doug Ford), annual taxes, second mortgages, et cetera – well, it all adds up.

I began to calculate which world destination we could have reached for the price of one week's stay at a cottage rental. And then I thought of many first-generation immigrants who would balk at the idea of spending their hard-earned, sacred North American dollars on a four-hour drive to an icy northern lake when these funds could be better earmarked for return trips to the homeland. But, of course, my husband and I are not first-generation immigrants looking longingly at the homeland our parents left behind. We are that curious breed born outside Canada and yet young enough to be absorbed into the cultural zeitgeist of our adopted land, so what was stopping us from breaking with one tradition and joining the ranks of another?

> *Get Your Fish On at Sandy Beach Cottage in North Bay*
> *A roomy cottage with sandy beach on secluded lake, three bedrooms, living, dining and full kitchen. Be ready to get your fish on at one of the best fishing spots around! Or feel free to make use of Paddle boat, canoe and two single Kayaks, with life jackets (4 universal, 1 XL, and 2 children sizes).*

Anthropology of the Cottage

RE: Get Your Fish On Reservation for Jun 20–30, 2021
Hello Jeff,
Your cottage sounds lovely! And we really appreciate the use of the paddle boat and other amenities you provide. Can you kindly confirm our reservation for the last week of June (occupation: 2).
Best,
Mariam

Hi Mariam,
Reservation confirmed. Looking forward to host you at our family cottage. I will send you the lock box combination and other details a few days before your planned arrival.
Thanks, Jeff

Looking forward, Jeff! And thanks for getting my name right!
Mariam

Not My American Dream

What is it about cottage ownership or cottage life that is so quintessentially Ontarian? What is it about the desire to hide out in the woods as soon as the rivers thaw and Victoria Day arrives that is so apparently appealing to Euro-Canadian settlers and so apparently unappealing to non-European émigré-settlers, many of whom are now multigenerational settlers in their own right? And don't just take my word for it! Freelance journalist Elamin Abdelmahmoud writes that "the cottage, as an idea, is spoken about with great reverence, but rarely by non-white immigrants."[5] Does this explain Harrison's point about the racial makeup of cottage country being relatively homogeneous, and her slightly less palatable discovery that at least for some of her interviewees the guaranteed "sameness" of cottage country was a euphemism for its whiteness?

Garden Inventories

We just have to look around cities like Toronto, Brampton, Scarborough and now even the outliers, like Waterloo, to know that Ontario receives the lion's share of new immigrants (disregard my family's trajectory to Nova Scotia, as my dear old dad was never known to follow the pack). The majority are thus urban, metropolitan beings by default, so perhaps this explains the relative "whiteness" of "up north." However, as the scientific credo goes, absence of evidence is not evidence of absence. Even Ronaldo and I take frequent day trips to enjoy the great outdoors in Ontario's innumerable conservation areas. Here, we have been pleasantly surprised to see large family gatherings that remind us of our respective *elsewheres* – that is, life before Canada – in the form of elaborate cookouts, garlicky lamb skewers sizzling on portable grills or desi dishes transported in large cauldrons, wafting through parks more accustomed to hotdog and hamburger barbecues. Granted, many of these POC (people of colour) sightings take place in the conservation areas closer to the Greater Toronto Area, such as Forks of the Credit or Heart Lake Conservation Park, but said encounters are no longer as unlikely as a run-in with a black bear.

However, the same cannot be said of cottage country. At least not yet, anyway. Indians – not the type of "Indians" found in Métis playwright Drew Hayden Taylor's *Cottagers and Indians*,[6] but my sort of Indians from the Indian subcontinent – are as much absent in those idyllic images of cottage life as they are excluded from the mythos of the Canadian wilderness and its itinerant pilgrimage from town to country, from primary home to summer home, from car to canoe. This may not be an active exclusion, but rather a symptom of new immigrant life. These new settlers tend to be caught up with the business of creating a first home, so the very idea of a *second* home (especially in one of the most inflated real estate markets in this hemisphere) hovers somewhere in the realm of absurdity, a mere blip among all the other summit-reaching feats that settling into a new land requires. And it is this absence, be it real or imagined, that makes me wonder: Does one need to own a cottage to, well, not so much to belong here, but to "make it" here? To make good on the American/Canadian dream?

Imagine my surprise when I learned that cottage ownership and, indeed, recreational land ownership, in Ontario's *el norte* was not a locally made, homespun idea like maple syrup or, my personal favourite, ketchup-flavoured chips. Cottage ownership was as foreign as Old Glory and the Liberty Bell. Yes, it was Canada's neighbours south of the border who first gravitated to that prime waterfront real estate hugging the Great Lakes. In the late nineteenth century, Ontario was selling land to wealthy Americans looking to build summer homes where they could indulge in back-to-nature getaways far from the madding American crowds. As Peter A. Stevens notes, by the early twentieth century Americans owned nearly 25 percent of lakefront property in the Muskoka region, and were equally well represented in Georgian Bay and as far east as the Thousand Islands on the St. Lawrence River.[7]

Ronaldo and I took one of those Thousand Islands boat tours a few summers ago, in our continued efforts to better acquaint ourselves with Ontario's geo-cultural landmarks. I might add that the Thousand Islands boat tour seems to stay afloat thanks to new immigrants looking for safe, preferably guided, access to the colossal waterways that make up so much of Canada's iconic wilderness. These fellow émigré-tourists nodded along, as we did, to the captain's informational broadcast. We learned that the largest and oldest recreational homes on this stretch of the St. Lawrence River were first built by wealthy American industrialists. This seems reasonable enough on a waterway that is also a riverine border between Canada and the United States, but I found my growing sense of

Canadian patriotism assaulted by the revelation that the Thousand Island dressing – that beautiful concoction I had always assumed to be, like ketchup chips, a distinctly Canadian food item – was likely commercialized by one of the more notable among these island residents: namely, George Boldt, proprietor of the Waldorf-Astoria hotel. Thousand Island dressing was, for my family, a Canadian food revelation, and to have it besmirched – nay, robbed – by some upstart from New York was the height of American cultural chauvinism!

These "summer homes" – be they built on the precarious islands dotting the mighty St. Lawrence River or along the rugged shorelines of the Great Lakes – were similarly tied to "foreigners" and, at least to some extent, imported ideas of leisure and recreation. They only started getting bound up with Canadian national symbols in the postwar period, when the Ontario government turned their sights on more local infusions of capital, a trend that continued up to 1967, Canada's centenary. However, by the time cottage country and Canadian national pride were to become synonymous for many Ontarians, the land grab had taken its toll, rendering such terrestrial dreams out of reach to all but the Canadian elite.

Grey Areas

If familial and cultural lore come to be shaped, in part, by cottage experience, which seems to take up a good chunk of the most clement months of the year, how are tropes of leisure, recreation and desire for the "great outdoors" similarly bound to this experience? Do diasporic Canadians risk further exclusion if they do not participate in or subscribe to these concepts of leisure? Should we, too, be getting out and about in the wilderness, which will no doubt do us smog-choked, often sedentary city-dwellers a world of good, but may also have other kinds of beneficial side effects, like the chance to assert our presence, stake our claim, insist that we, too, belong not only here in the urban jungle, but also here on the Precambrian rocks of the Muskokas, and here in the boreal forests of the Kawarthas, names that call out to some like an old family quilt, familiar and inviting, and to others like a Group of Seven painting, exotic and unattainable. And if we are to embrace cottage experience, how does this not capitulate into another colonizing act of Indigenous lands and waters, and the cultures and histories rooted there for millennia? Are we simply to be wedged between competing narratives of settlement and displacement? How did my plans for a summer staycation get so damn complicated?

Some might say that cottage landownership is mired in colonial practices and their legacy. This was driven home to us in a casual conversation with a contractor we hired to renovate our bathroom in the summer of 2020, when having a "masked" stranger in one's home was suddenly deemed safe. Our contractor (let's call him Bryan) complained that he wouldn't be able to get up to his lakefront cottage that summer. The obstacle, he explained, was the First Nation band council, who were not permitting entry to cottage owners. I speculated that the First Nations might be exercising extra caution, extending quarantine beyond Public Health guidelines, given their historic plight as a people once ravaged by disease-carrying agents and other acts of biological warfare, but Bryan wasn't particularly moved by matters of history that essentially came down to, in his words, the fact that the "natives had lost the war." Naturally, I wanted to argue the point but thought better of it – my bathroom reno was still underway and we had already vetted numerous contractors and heard enough horror stories to know that we had hit the contractor-jackpot. Gross historical and racial biases notwithstanding, Bryan was personable, ethical, reliable, professional and highly skilled. So I probed further into Bryan's conundrum and learned that his cottage was built on land leased out by the First Nations based on what was known as "conditional land surrender" for recreational purposes.

Land in the Reserves is, to date, far cheaper than on Crown land, but comes with the caveat that it is available by lease only. Outsiders can own the house they build but not the land it stands on. This could be seen as a win for cottagers like Bryan looking to break into an exorbitant real estate market, and also for First Nations communities such as the Saugeen Ojibway, whose land sits along some of Lake Huron's most desirable shoreline, looking to capitalize on that market. However, these cottagers sign a lease with the knowledge that it might not be renewed at the time of expiry, and some have been known to refuse to vacate properties at the time of an expired lease, resulting in ugly and costly legal battles.[8] It's still a pretty sweet deal though, considering some leases, like Bryan's, are good for a whopping ninety-nine years.

So far be it for me to paint a binary picture of landownership in cottage country. It is, like the gneiss and granite rocks of Georgian Bay and the Bruce Peninsula, another kind of grey area. However, Bryan's situation makes me even more curious about where this overwhelming desire to possess a piece of the proverbial Canadian Shield comes from. We might say it is grounded in a very human and universal desire to connect with nature. But spaces designated as "natural" or unspoiled might also be seen as social constructs rooted in some less than savoury imperialist machinations. At least in Ontario, we need look no further than the landscape paintings of the Group of Seven, of which I am a self-confessed fan. In these gorgeous representations of northern Ontario, fantasy, mythology and colonialism coalesce in the making of Canada's "wilderness"

Anthropology of the Cottage

portrait.⁹ Be it in the works of Tom Thomson, synonymous with the sublime interiors of Algonquin Park where he briefly worked as a fire ranger for a logging company, or those of Lawren Harris, who visually abstracted the icescapes of Lake Superior, there is generally not a person or man-made structure in sight. Of course, these painters were singularly focused on the more remote northern spaces of Ontario, but as Patricia Jasen reminds us in her fascinating study *Wild Things: Nature, Culture, and Tourism in Ontario, 1790–1914*, the wilderness of these areas is only *un*inhabited by virtue of the ways land was wrestled out of Indigenous control for the purposes of white settlement and the tourist industry.¹⁰ Peter A. Stevens reinforces this point, saying the term *cottage country* only gained currency after World War II when it came to imply, "without much geographical specificity," a recreational hinterland devoid of all groups but the recreationists.¹¹ Granted, the Group of Seven also tend to exclude said recreationists from their paintings, but you get my point: at least in these early iterations of cottage country, the fact that this hinterland was also a place of "work, industry, and permanent local populations, including First Nations," seems wholly and perhaps insistently irrelevant.¹²

When a leaky faucet required Bryan's expert follow-up, we had the opportunity to see our loquacious handyman again.

"So, did I tell you I've moved?" he announced giddily. "I live by Durham now."

A fumbling scroll through Google Maps popped up Durham in Grey County, located about an hour and a half north of Waterloo, which situated Bryan a hundred kilometres closer to his cottage along the inlets and coves of southern Georgian Bay.

When Bryan showed us a satellite image of the hundred-acre property he'd purchased there, I had to gasp. "You must have your own lake out in a property that size!"

"Actually, there is a river running through the property . . . And I've got the permit to set up an ATV track – you know, like an adventure park! I mean, I've got to generate some income up there."

"Wow!" I tried to keep up. How had we leaped from a *river runs through it* to *ATV adventure parks*?

"So no more cottage, then?" Ronaldo asked.

"Oh no! We still get up to the cottage! Now more than ever!"

Bryan was working his way northward, to a permanent stake in cottage country, one-hundred-year lease at a time, one hundred acres at a time, one bathroom reno at a time.

Space Invaders

I'm a child of the seventies and a teen of the eighties. Like many kids of my generation, I was hooked on video games played at arcades or on household Atari consoles. *Space Invaders* was a personal favourite. I could feel my heart race every time the aliens, modelled after crabs and squids, dropped down a line, closing in on their target – namely, me, the lone virtual player represented by a single cannon firing against a relentless alien invasion. It didn't matter who or what the aliens were. Only their annihilation mattered in a game of kill or be killed. I wonder if, in that matrix of combat, I was priming myself for a life committed to studying the history of colonization, which has, more often than not, played itself out like a dystopian fiction.[13]

Alternately, I can't help but see the irony in this skewed self-image as a territorial defender, since I have spent most of my life in the position of the alien-invader entering someone else's airspace, settling on someone else's land. Nowhere was this more apparent than in the England of the '70s and early '80s when questions of

Anthropology of the Cottage

citizenship were subjects of great debate among British parliamentarians. Under the auspices of Margaret Thatcher's Conservative government, these debates culminated in the historic British Nationality Act of 1981, which effectively removed, to those formerly deemed "British subjects" or members of the Commonwealth, the historic right of residency in the United Kingdom. And just like that the tables were turned: the invaded (those once colonized in their own lands) becometh invaders ("undesirable" immigrants in the West).

My father was not a patient man. He was not one to ride out a storm, though in all fairness we had lived in England a good six years – an eternity for any persons of colour holding out for the prospect of citizenship in a racially charged political environment. Always driven by a tragic degree of hubris, I can just hear him now: "If they don't want us, we don't want them!" After a childhood spent in merry old England, my Queen's English and I were on a reverse trajectory to Pakistan. But it didn't take long for my father to realize that this was not the Pakistan of the '70s he had left behind. This was the Pakistan of the '80s, and it had moved into the future without him. In both homeland and host-land we were no longer recognizable to others, much less to ourselves. We were the foreigners in the room. The people on the ground held us in their line of sight, cannons locked into position, and we were suspended between two worlds, like those pixelated squids and crabs, wondering where we could run for cover. We had become moving targets as perennial space invaders, first in England, then "back" in Pakistan and soon enough in the United Arab Emirates, the Philippines and eventually Canada, where we arrived as "landed immigrants" in 1987. And the funny thing about space invaders is their acute awareness of . . . well, space. Space invaders may come to inhabit a space – even love the space they inhabit – but they don't, for a minute, take that space for granted. Because no space is a birthright. No space is home turf. And to use a sports metaphor that is as alien to me as the galaxy itself, no space provides the home advantage.

Of course, the "up north" (or cottage country) of Ontario has been, by and large, a space of twoness – rivalling dualities between Indigenous and white settler – but if there's one thing the COVID-19 pandemic has achieved it is drawing out Canadian urbanites of all races and places to cottage country, be it as digital nomads looking for a quiet place to work, or a new generation of Ontarians realizing that a shoebox condo in the city is not the optimum place to be when the next pandemic hits. But how will this new breed of space invader behave? I, for one, would not wish to add any more fuel, be it aerial or terrestrial, to the fires that Indigenous peoples have been struggling to put out for the last five hundred years. After all, my own ancestors have shared some of that struggle, our own families' Partition and post-Partition displacements an adequate reminder of the British Empire's legacy. At the same time, I recognize that I am here. This puts me in the unusual position of a double space invader. A two-timing space invader, of sorts.

Perhaps for this reason I have come to see myself not as an immigrant but as an émigré-settler. That is, I am both another kind of settler – a space invader par excellence – in Indigenous lands, as well as something other: the squid, the crab, the alien being fired at from below. On the one hand, I don't wish to be seen as that invading force and thus resist the urge to stake a claim in lands and ecologies – botanical, biological, social and cultural – already in distress. On the other hand, I cannot escape the fact of my arrival. Of my own "landed immigrant" status, to adopt official parlance. And now, with our house in Waterloo, as a landowner.

Anthropology of the Cottage

Re: Cancellation request at Get Your Fish On for June 20–30, 2021
Hello Jeff,
Unfortunately, we are not going to make it to your beautiful cottage, and request a refund.

Hi Mariam,
AirBnB should be able to help you with the refund process.
Thanks,
Jeff

Eating Precambrian Humble Pie

Ronaldo's birthday falls on June 21, the summer solstice. He was definitely starting to show signs of cabin fever after a year of total lockdown. And how did I respond? Like a good partner, I got onto my computer and started googling stuff. Specifically, cabins! Or rather, cottages. At least a trip to cottage country would get us out of the house, even though it would actually just get us out of *our* house, with its many creature comforts, and put us into a *stranger's* house, with only the bare necessities. But it would still be an excursion – something special to look forward to for his birthday. At least we could join the exodus north and see what all the fuss was about, first-hand. So, like a well-trained academic, I researched: areas, cottage types (independent, resort, family-oriented, et cetera), distances, rates and availability. I narrowed my search and contacted the top three prospective cottage rentals on my list. Most were clustered around the Muskokas, in eastern Georgian Bay, since I was curious about this most celebrated of regions. As it turned out, I ended up reserving a cottage in the North Bay area. I liked it for a number of reasons: It was close enough to Georgian Bay but far enough to get better bang for your buck. It was also an area

Garden Inventories

largely under the territorial control of First Nations communities, such as the Dokis First Nation. I liked the fact Indigenous business owners, interpreters, guides and artists could be our gateway to the north. I found an independent cottage on a lake with its own private beach, and well-stocked with hinterland gear, life jackets, paddleboats, kayaks and canoes. It seemed too good to be true: Why was such a nice place still available at a relatively reasonable price, when campsites and cottages were in such high demand that people were making reservations a year in advance? No matter! I paid the full price to secure my reservation, and tried to generate some excitement about our own special trip "up north."

A change in scenery would do us a world of good, I professed, even though my anxious inner voice was working overtime: What would we actually *do* at this cottage for seven straight days? We are avidly average hikers but the thought of bear encounters still fills me with terror. We liked the outdoors but my rheumatoid condition did not take well to damp evenings spent under the stars. Moreover, in late June (which stands in as the frigid first week of summer) even a toe would contract hypothermia in such glacial waters. We also anticipated having to pack quite a bit of "stuff" at a time when restaurants and other outlets may very well have gone out of business or were still functioning with limited stock. None of the usual Indigenous festivals or even touristy activities, few and far between as they were, were going to be running during the pandemic, so nature would have to be our number one entertainment source.

Still, I was determined. If not now, then when? So we opened our virtual maps and started looking for the best route to our newly secured cottage rental in the environs of Lake Nipissing, the largest body of water in North Bay. Google Maps indicated that it would be a 403-kilometre trip from Waterloo to Lake Nipissing,

Anthropology of the Cottage

and would take approximately four hours, not including traffic. I should mention here that my husband and I used to drive the five hours between Waterloo, Ontario, and Montreal, Quebec, almost every other weekend in the first year we moved to Waterloo, so it wasn't as if we were skittish about long road trips. And yet, the almost-equivalent distance and time invested in getting from one little pocket of Ontario to another little, even remoter pocket of Ontario still left me scratching my head. Was it worth it? And yet, wasn't the proverbial road trip itself – all these highways and byways that made *el norte* the car owner's paradise – an indelible feature of the Great White North adventure?

My enthusiasm was rebooted and I surfed the net for more information about our cottage destination, when I came across an article (article upon article, actually) about the shadfly in North Bay. I had never heard of shadflies. I was well aware of blackflies and mosquitos – the memory of a raging swarm preventing us from setting foot outdoors at a colleague's cottage still sends me running for the calamine lotion. But these shadflies were something else. They are *Jurassic Park* big (okay, they are a few millimetres long but the Mesozoic era still comes to mind). And they come out in such inestimably large swarms that size really doesn't matter! They appear in undulating blankets of terror, covering lampposts, cars, docks – entire towns! Locals have to "shovel" them off their driveways like black snow! And those same shadfly-victimized locals have been known to take pleasure in seeing tourists run for their lives from a shadfly swarm. Apparently, some comfort is to be taken in the fact that these creatures don't bite because they have "no mouths." The horror!

Some locals say shadfly season erupts in the first weeks of July (when they emerge from the lakes in a mating frenzy), and others say they could appear around the end of June, and that shadfly

Garden Inventories

season can last anywhere from two to four weeks! I almost fainted! Shadfly season could take up our entire staycation in and around North Bay! No wonder the people in the know (those Ontarians born and raised) had not reserved this idyllic cottage at this seemingly rock-bottom price! I scrambled to cancel our reservation. Fortunately, it was early enough to get my two thousand dollars back in full. I felt bad for the cottage owner, but not too bad, considering he hadn't bothered to say a word about "shadfly season"! I also felt a tinge of sadness letting go of my albeit fleeting cottage dream, but I talked us into an alternative and perhaps less harrowing weekend excursion to commemorate another milestone, our twenty-first wedding anniversary. We married in August so this would put us well out of the reach of shadfly season. And if this alone did not seal the deal, then a stay at a good old-fashioned bed and breakfast in Parry Sound seemed more appealing than a week holed up in a stranger's house in the shadfly-infested woods.

In a final sales pitch to Ronaldo, I mentioned Parry Sound's proximity to the historically significant French River, which connects Lake Nipissing to Georgian Bay, but seeing as this park is best experienced from a kayak or a canoe, sightseeing for the landbound is restricted to an eight-kilometre roundtrip hike, which we completed in record time. This left us with little else to do, bereft of the skills and equipment that others who grow up with summer camp or cottage experience take for granted. So on our drive back to Parry Sound we headed to Killbear Provincial Park where we got into a classic couples' tiff about directions, and ended up on the wrong trail. The lookout point across the bay was nice enough but it wasn't the trail I had set my sights on – the trail that apparently culminated at the windswept, right-leaning lone Jack pine made famous by Group of Seven's Frederick H. Varley's *Stormy Weather, Georgian Bay* painting.

Anthropology of the Cottage

Oh well. I consoled myself with some Group of Seven souvenirs purchased at a lovely gift shop in Parry Sound. So it wasn't a cottage experience, I shrugged. So it was only a weekend at a B&B where we weren't even served "breakfast" because the proprietors weren't ready to recommit to indoor dining. Any form of leisure was a gift at a time when so many were suffering the personal, financial and other losses created by the pandemic. So, with said gratitude in mind, we made the most of it. Apparently, there were boat tours of "the world's largest freshwater archipelago" clustered around Georgian Bay, though our tour-boat captain efficiently sped us past a mere fraction of the whopping *thirty* thousand islands publicized in the *Island Queen* brochure. At least the tour included a pit stop at an island diner that was something of an institution for the cottage-owning, speedboat-riding non-local locals but, as these things go, we were served up a grossly overpriced lunch consisting of farmed perch. At least we got to eat some locally caught fish, I sighed, only to learn that the perch was imported from Lake Erie, closer to OUR neck of the woods! This was not, in other words, either the romantic anniversary outing I had imagined nor the cottage experience I had formerly planned. But it was a wobbly baby step into the Great White North, wasn't it? And in spite of the aching feet and imported fish and chips, as well as the quarantine-addled brains of an otherwise harmonious couple, we hope to take our next adventure even farther north. I'm thinking Lake Superior–north and, who knows, even Pickle Lake!

A small, parting confession: I stole something while we were up in *el norte's el norte*. More like poached. Yes, in colonial backwoodsman hunting parlance, I, too, *came, saw and poached* something from the French River Provincial Park grounds. Before you call the animal welfare society, my hunting trophy did not move about on four legs. In fact, it seemed quite immovable where it lay

Garden Inventories

among its kin, in a heap of quarried granite. Okay, so some would call this heap a central feature of the landscaping but surely one teeny-weeny, pomelo-sized geological specimen won't be missed in a place where rock – megatons and megatons of Precambrian igneous rock – has dominated the Canadian shield for four billion years!

My teeny-weeny rock is, like most rocks, distinctly grey. But, like the signature of the region's bedrock, it is decorated with a pinkish-orange stripe, almost as if it's been kissed by the salmon on their annual migrations, from river to sea or, in this case, to a lake as big as some seas. The rock sparkles when the sunlight hits it, out in the garden where I placed it among the rudbeckias and sedums. It is something to be admired, this glittery sliver of Georgian Bay. It is a humbling thing – this little slice of Precambrian pie.

Garden Inventories

A species can be considered native if it occurred in the region before human settlement introduced non-native species from other areas. Local native species are often called "indigenous"... Non-native species can sometimes coexist with native species without becoming a problem. Concerns arise when a non-native species becomes invasive.[1]

Ten Thousand Steps

COVID locked us in and pushed us out. Out into our neighbourhoods. Out into the green spaces beyond the walls of our confinement. My solitary walks around the neighbourhood became walks of companionship with Ronaldo, when lockdown also coincided with his first year of retirement. I've dubbed Ronaldo the Mountain Man, because he was born in Huehuetenango, on the volcanic slopes of western Guatemala. My Mountain Man was not content with what I considered a decent average of four thousand walking steps per day. For me, four thousand steps consisted of my preferred loop from our house, down into Colonial Creek (a "conservation space" serving as a stormwater drainage system emptying out into the Grand River) and back out again into our neighbourhood. Ronaldo needed more steps if these walks were going to substitute for his badminton games, now off-limits during quarantine, so we ventured into a newer development that sits on the north side of Colonial Creek. This led us to a path wrapping around a school and a few deserted "green spaces" – basically, fields reserved for baseball games nobody ever seems to play – and up toward another school and another field backing into a wooded area. Four thousand steps covered and we weren't even beginning to loop back home! I was about to protest but Mountain Man with his cabra-legs said, "Look, there's a path into the woods! Don't you want to see where it goes?" I did but my own Jell-O-legs resisted. I had to agree that a forest in the middle of a sprawling housing development was a thing of wonder, so I suppressed a big fat no and followed him into the woods.

It was all so still. So quiet. So big. So green. I was Alice taking a first step into Wonderland. Curiouser and curiouser, I was filled with questions, like why would developers, programmed like a Marvel comic book hero to raze everything in their path, leave so much prime real estate untouched?

Mountain Man, also often dubbed Zen Master for a mindful disposition before *mindfulness* was a buzzword, said, "Just enjoy it for what it is."

We're not forest newbies, Ronaldo and I. We were starting to ramp up our hiking expeditions to get better acquainted with Ontario, and we'd both lived in semi-rural areas in our premarital lives – Ronaldo in northern Quebec and myself in the peri-urban outskirts of Halifax. But to come upon a forest mere steps away from home – well, about five thousand steps from our door, according to Fitbit – was, indeed, worth some mindful reflection. And with nothing but time to return to it, day after day, for four consecutive seasons in lockdown, it gave us a lot of Zen credits, not to mention a daily tally of ten thousand steps.

An interpretive sign at the edge of the woods referred to our new discovery as a "woodlot," meaning it didn't quite make the cut as a full-fledged forest and functioned as little more than a trail for dog walkers or kids looking to take a shortcut home from school. But as far as deciduous woodland goes, it provided respite from barren, treeless fields and the visual vacuity of the suburbs. Soon enough, we were charging along baseball fields and deserted school grounds (thanks to quarantine) with the promise

of cherished walks through this "woodlot." Once inside, our steps and our heart rate slowed, our chest cavities widened and the joyful work of noticing began. At first, we were snapping pictures of tree canopies for something to post on Facebook. Then the cameras started to turn downward, and our attention became less about the number of "likes" our cool shots would generate than about the discovery of all that vegetation beneath and around our feet. Suddenly, we were transported from the twenty-first to the nineteenth century, following in the pioneering footsteps of Catharine Parr Traill, early colonial settler and naturalist, as we took mental field notes of New World flora, eager to report how these "forest glades and boggy swamps hide away many a rare and precious flower known to but a few."² But unlike Traill, we had Google Lens at our disposal.

Snap and a quick Google Lens search later, I learned some names: burdock.

Snap: mayapple.

Snap: yellow trout lily.

Snap: chokecherry.

Snap: Canada anemone.

Snap: bloodroot.

As he continued exploring the land, Nanabozho [or Nanabush, the Anishinaabeg spiritual and trickster figure] was given a new responsibility: to learn the names of all the beings. He watched them carefully to see how they lived and spoke with them to learn what gifts they carried in order to discern their true names. Right away he began to feel more at home and was not lonely anymore when he could call the others by name and they called out to him when he passed.³

Through the Looking Glass

COVID quarantining also gave us a lot of time to look inward – that is, at the walls, floors, nooks and crannies of our homes. How quickly these edifices drawn from a contractor's infinitely reproducible blueprint become individuated expressions of ourselves. Our early occupation of a home unfolds like a reality home reno TV show. In record time, we strip things bare, we tear things down and the more ambitious among us even put sledgehammers to walls and floors. In our house, we had neither the time nor the budget for quite so drastic a demolition, but we were no less guilty of scrambling to erase our predecessors' footprints. This meant peeling away

Garden Inventories

layers of wallpaper, ripping out putrid shades of vinyl flooring and piles of baby blue carpet – Benjamin Moore not being quite the colour connoisseur it is now – all the hallmarks of 1980s décor. Then and only then could the work of reoccupation begin, as if even so much as the whiff of another's presence somehow makes a house that much less of a home. To be fair, we lived with those melamine countertops and Hollywood dressing-room lights for far longer than I would have liked, and our basement still suffers both an aesthetic and functionary identity crisis (moonlighting as home office, gym, guest room and makeshift art studio), but I'm sure our house would be quite unrecognizable, perhaps even inhospitable, to its previous occupants now.

It takes time for such impulses – at lease for those of us who do our own landscaping – to spill over into the more natural, albeit equally circumscribed, space of the garden. But eventually we go there. And even if we don't immediately take our demolition hats to the space just beyond our windows, we do spend time cogitating and critiquing how we're going to make that garden after our own image as well. Every time I wash the dishes I have nothing to do but take a mental inventory of this little plot of land, with all its possible subtractions and additions. Our gardens, too, become expressions of ourselves, be it in their nurturing or their neglect, be it in the plants we add or the plants we take away, and the very ideas we bring along about space and land and place itself. While our houses are quickly refurnished and filled with the noises and smells of our lives, our territories marked and claimed like the neighbour's dog repeatedly pissing on our Jack pines, our gardens are slower to remove our predecessors' muddy footprints. But once we focus on what the garden might say about the people who had once put down roots before us, it, too, opens itself up like that wondrous woodlot, and the process of inventory-taking and intimate knowing begins.

Garden Inventories

I'm ashamed to say that it has taken me as much time to look – really look – at our garden as it took to really look at those "natural" spaces beyond it. Life just always got in the way. Ronaldo and I had to live apart for the first two years of our relocation to Waterloo. I arrived in 2005 to take up my tenure-track appointment in the Department of English and Film Studies at Wilfrid Laurier University, and Ronaldo stayed behind in Montreal to basically wrap up a twenty-five-year career as a college professor of computer science in the Quebec CÉGEP system. He joined me one year after we bought our home in east Waterloo, where he quickly found a position as research support staff at the Cheriton School of Computer Science at the University of Waterloo. As a university town, Waterloo also proved to be a curious place: the entire city grows and shrinks in population like a party balloon at the beginning and end of each academic year, and it seemed that at least half the personnel, faculty and staff at each of our universities were commuters who lived elsewhere. To further compound the kind of transience felt in such a place, academic life involves quite a bit of travel, for conferencing, for field research, for networking and even just because of the mobility long summers unhitched to an office job provide.

The garden was secondary to our busy lives. We dabbled in it from time to time, planting a tree or extending a bed, and eventually doing away with an enormous deck in a culture obsessed with decks for reasons I have as yet to understand. I mean, all that wood consumption is hard on the environment, it is a costly beast to maintain after sitting under ice and snow five months of the year, and it wedges itself between house and garden like a schoolyard bully. Every time I stood atop our three-tiered deck, I felt like Kate Winslet on the bow of the *Titanic*. There is a place and purpose for it in homes built at higher elevations, like an alpine summit or the

Garden Inventories

Canadian Rockies, but its utility on a piece of land as flat as the Salar de Uyuni just made no sense to me.

Saving up funds to tear down the deck and put a stone patio in its place was like that very first step into the woodlot. When we stepped out into the garden, we were level with it. We were part of it. We weren't looking down our noses at it. And suddenly, it started to see us too. It sang its secrets. Of the life before our arrival. Before settlement. And its struggles and triumphs of growth ever since.

By now a master of Google Lens, I started to make lists. First, mental lists, and then proper records of the garden, then and now. Then – that is, the garden as it was when we first moved in – the garden inventory looked something like this:

- Trees: Jack pines (numerous). Two white ash trees (now removed because of their demise at the hands of emerald ash borer disease). One mountain ash (aka Siberian mountain ash). European buckthorns (far too many to count).

- Woody Plants/Shrubs: Euonymus (a few varieties like burning bush). Weigela. Holly. Dappled willow. Rose. Hydrangea. Concord grape. Purpleleaf sand cherry.

- Herbaceous Perennials: Day lily. Peony. Hosta. Clematis. Lungwort. Forget-me-not. Lily of the valley. Periwinkle. More roses.

- And neither herbaceous perennial nor shrub, but in a league of its own: The ostrich fern.

The garden was clearly as low on variety as it was in aesthetics. But before I got as judgy as an Instagramming adolescent, I tried to take stock of our own planting:

Garden Inventories

- Trees: American horse chestnut. White pines (numerous). Some type of fir. Apple. Crabapple. Mulberry. Japanese maple. Crimson queen Japanese maple.

- Evergreen Shrubs: Yew. Cypress. Juniper. Mugo pine.

- Woody Plants/Shrubs: Lilacs. Barberry. Smoke Bush. Spirea. Rose of Sharon. Sedum. Lavender. Yucca.

- Spring Bulbs: Allium. Iris. *Muscari*. Hyacinth. Daffodil (a flower flogged in English colonial curricula, from Bombay to Barbados, and as emblematic of the English countryside as they come – that is, if John Keats's vision of golden daffodils "fluttering and dancing in the breeze" is anything to go by).

Again, not an overwhelming list, but at least we were edging toward a stronger palette, variety and four-seasonal interest. However, Monty Dons or Marjorie Harrises we certainly were not and our plant selections were made in the most haphazard of ways: something was on sale at the nursery (the makeshift kind erected in big box store parking lots, just to make Joni Mitchell mad with the irony!); or we spotted something we liked in a neighbour's garden; or we remembered something our mothers may have planted in the many gardens they had tended over the years.

There was a troubling imbalance in our garden, as well: while some things grew with unrelenting vigour, like the buckthorns running along an unruly back border, other things tended to look sickly or lost amid weeds – or, at least, what we identified as weeds at the time because we couldn't seem to keep them under control. Following our neighbours' lead, we mulched in May, we added topsoil and we weeded, weeded, weeded. But something just wasn't right. As if no matter what we did to turn our garden into a subject worthy of a Monet painting, all we ever ended up with was a garage-sale forgery. A poor imitation of a garden.

Garden Inventories

The more we walked along the creek and through the woodlot the more I realized that my garden inventory bore absolutely no resemblance to the inventory of flora I was discovering in these more natural habitats. And as for the garden we inherited, it didn't reflect our own tastes much at all. For one, that mess of buckthorns and Jack pines at the plot's perimeter took up a whole lot of space and light and air. There was a Concord grapevine hogging a prime location where I would have much preferred a ballroom of flowers dancing in the sunlight. The giant hostas were magnificent but demanded far greater room than a mangy corner bed allowed. The clematises lost their support along the by-now demolished old deck's trellised hull,  and a few stubborn rose bushes insisted on surviving the trauma of transplantation.

I consulted Google Lens, this time snapping photos of our own garden ornamentals. I was horrified to discover that most of our shrubbery, trees and flowers would be classified as "non-native." In fact, even in the non-native category, many of our plant selections fell decidedly on the side of "invasive" species. Our garden was the site of multiple invasions – floral, herbaceous, evergreen, woody, grassy, annual, biennial and perennial! Our garden was under siege and we were the generals overseeing the invasion!

Non-native species can be aggressive or vigorous growers and can overwhelm and outcompete the local native species. This upsets the natural balance and results in the loss of the native species and sometimes whole communities, thereby lowering the overall biodiversity and health of an area. Invasive plants can lower biodiversity so greatly that they create a monotypic community (where the invasive species is the only plant growing). An invasive species is an organism that grows and spreads quickly because it can adapt to a variety of growing conditions. Invasive species are often non-native (introduced from other areas) and lack the usual predators that control their population.[4]

Conservation Efforts

A generous patch of woodland in a suburban development is a protected area. This, in turn, implies there is something worth protecting therein. Something to be conserved. And conservation efforts tend to kick in when something is already at risk. When we took the time to read the "Eastbridge Woodlot" interpretive sign, our sense that sugar maple trees dominated the forest was confirmed; the sign also made us aware of a "regionally rare tree species, [the] rock elm (*Ulmus thomasii*)," as well as numerous kinds of ground cover for which to be on the lookout. The mention of the elusive

Garden Inventories

rock elm begged the question: What other rare or at-risk species did these woodlots and other "natural" habitats contain? If histories of conquest are anything to go by, at-risk species are, in the best-case scenario, threatened or displaced by the overpopulation of other species, as the dominant sugar maples suggested; in the worst-case scenario, they are forcibly removed or eradicated from their native habitats. One might say that even immigrants from once colonized lands, such as my parents, have been driven out of their natal habitats, becoming denizens and transplants in non-native habitats, sometimes of their choosing (choice being relative to circumstance) and sometimes not. Any ethnocultural group from a conquered place has been rendered an at-risk species at some point in the historical continuum, so why would ecological communities escape such a fate?

It was clear that such natural habitats held the key to my garden woes, because surely whatever grew there, be it in a state of depletion or dominance, was *of this place*. Whatever grew there had been "protected" against eradication by the developer's bulldozer or the gardener's trowel. Out there I could do away with the treacherous business of names and simply trust the veracity of my own eyes. Out there I could take a visual inventory and compare it to my own garden inventory. I could start telling the difference between native and non-native species and, in so doing, get to the bottom of my garden's ill health.

Mountain Man and I laced up our sneakers, reset Fitbit and returned to the creeks and woodlands, not only to get in our ten thousand steps but also to look and notice things *sans* Google Lens. Soon enough, the land was telling us stories in the way our garden was yielding its secrets, along with some of its complaints. And every season told us a different story. In the late spring and early summer months we were amazed by the number of flowering trees and shrubs to be found around the creek. Some even filled the suburban air with perfumes that could easily compete with the headiest of tropical flowers. One such tree was worthy of note in my journal, which read something like this: "The linden tree (aka basswood or *Tilia*) is neither showy in form nor stature. But it produces a profusion of flowers at the tips of delicate stems that break out into constellations, like pale yellow and white starbursts. The scent is often described as a mixture of honey and lemon but it reminds me of jasmines, so that's how I'm going to think of the linden flowers now: the jasmines of the north."

The woodlot also had a diversity of stories to tell. For one, the grounds were carpeted with trillium – branded Ontario's official floral emblem during the First World War – as well as a host of other woodland gems. These early forest-dwelling spring bloomers, such hopeful symbols in a bitterly cold climate, are all too easily crushed under a winter boot. And yet they can easily rival the crocus bulbs we are programmed to plant in our gardens. One such rival to the ubiquitous crocus appeared in the form of a nodding yellow flower with mottled green leaves, the latter characteristic lending itself to the wholly ugly name of yellow trout lily (I mean, who names a flower after a fish!). This yellow trout lily appeared about the same time as my crocus was bursting through the snow, but while the crocus was an import easily procured from dollar stores to Walmarts to the fancier nurseries, the native yellow trout lily hadn't made the commercial leap, it would seem, from wildflower to garden flower.

In fact, many of the things we took a mental and visual note of in these natural habitats were hard to come by in the commercial nursery industry, from shrubs like the pepperbush, winterberry and highbush cranberry to a spectrum of flowering plants, including wild geranium, wild bergamot, wild columbine, yellow iris, marsh marigold, hyssop, cardinal flower, purple loosestrife . . . I suppose the majority of these flowers and shrubs would be perceived, if not classified, as "wild" around here, which gives one the impression that "wild" and "native" plant species are synonymous. But there was also trickery afoot because some of these plants, like yellow iris and loosestrife, which were clearly thriving in the wild were *not*, in fact, native to this region – they were not even native to Canada! They were decidedly *non-native* species that appeared to have infiltrated *native* camps. If, as former Prime Minister Jean Chrétien once said, "A proof is a proof . . . and when you have a good proof it's because it's proven," we were amassing plenty of good proof that something was just not adding up in these "conservation" areas.

And this something was nowhere better exemplified than in the form of the European buckthorn, aka common buckthorn, aka *Rhamnus cathartica*.

Common Buckthorn is native to Europe and is also known as European Buckthorn. In Canada, it is found from Nova Scotia to Saskatchewan. It was likely introduced around the 1880s, becoming widespread in the early 1900s. This species was often used in hedgerows and windbreaks, and was widely planted across the country. . . .

. . . It is now found throughout southern Ontario and grows in a wide range of habitats, spreading rapidly along roadsides, fence lines, woodland edges, and in pastures and abandoned fields. Buckthorn fruit has a laxative effect on wildlife which helps to widely distribute the seeds.

Common Buckthorn invasions can harm the economy and the environment. It out-competes native plants, reduces biodiversity, degrades the quality of wildlife habitat, and impacts a wide range of industries.[5]

Garden Inventories

Battle of Waterloo

The gloves were off. This was war. For so many years the buckthorns lined up against our back fence like an infantry battalion had tricked us into believing they belonged here – that, like any decent ally, they were doing us a service, protecting us from air pollution and traffic noise while giving local fauna much-needed shelter and perhaps even a healthy snack. We assumed their little black berries provided sustenance though they mostly fell on the ground, unpalatable to furry and feathery fauna alike. They were hardy enough, their leaves staying green well past the expiration date of other deciduous trees in our borrowed landscape – those trees in our neighbours' gardens, like maple, beech, oak and birch. Ronaldo had already started to tire of the number of saplings they spawned, both from seed and a network of roots, grumbling they were taking over the garden. But it was only when we came across buckthorns in the Eastbridge Woodlot that we knew something was rotten in the state of our garden.

In the woodlot we just had to notice this shrubby tree's hawkish temperament. Like Napoleon's troops it flanked the forest's perimeter, and had even managed to infiltrate its central chamber. And like anyone foolish enough to underestimate the French emperor, mistaking the buckthorn's lower stature, at least in the vertical hierarchy of trees, as a sign of weakness was a strategic error with dire consequences. Because the buckthorn's power lay in its horizontal arsenal: a mesh of vine-like branches holding an entire forest in a sun-deprived chokehold. How could something so self-aggrandizing be part of this native habitat, we wondered? In whose interest was it to conserve this marauding army of buckthorns when it was clear that it was on an imperialist mission to vanquish everything in its path? In a place where there should have been black walnuts and oaks and beeches and hemlocks, only sugar maples and ashes (at least those left standing after the emerald ash borer epidemic) remained as a last line of defence against the encroaching buckthorn.[6] And the buckthorn was fast accruing foliate supremacy, from scrappy shrub to understorey tree to the forest's dominant canopy.

On our next walk we stopped to reread the Eastbridge Woodlot sign, hoping to better understand the buckthorn's role in this forest ecosystem, but there was no mention of the tree. We could only deduce that the buckthorn was either a non-native species or a native species that stood out like a sore thumb, like the sugar maple, because of the depopulation of other native species. To be fair, there are also homes backing directly onto this green space, which means the buckthorn could have easily leapt from some of these gardens into the woodlot. Or had it leapt from the woodlot into neighbouring gardens? Either way, we were disheartened to discover that this woodlot, where buckthorns and sugar maples shoved and pushed the other kids on the block, was hardly an exemplary model of biodiversity or native flora.

I perused the City of Waterloo's bylaw 08-026, *Respecting the Conservation of Trees in Woodlands*, which stipulates, "Except as otherwise provided in this By-law, no person shall destroy or injure a tree, or cause another person to destroy or injure a tree, of a protected species that is located in a woodland."[7] Such woodlands are thus viewed, in the language of human governance, as clearly demarcated areas, as if nature ever gave a crap about borders and boundaries. Perhaps the city had just missed the botanical memo: the surveyor's boundary line between controlled landscapes and "natural" landscapes is as arbitrary and mythical as the line demarcating the United States and Canada (or that giant ice wall in *Game of Thrones*). It is erected with the hubris of those who believe that nature, like people, can be divided and contained. Tell that to George R.R. Martin's super-soldiering Night's Watch defending a seven-hundred-foot, three-hundred-mile-wide monstrosity against . . . some equally monstrous "others"!

So let's just say the plot thickened: What, precisely, was being conserved within the vegetative walls of this suburban woodlot? And what kind of template did such circumscribed spaces provide for novice gardeners like ourselves, hoping to learn a little bit more about the land on the other side of this invisible wall, this protected native habitat? Who was on the "inside" and who on the "outside"? Weren't we breathing the same air as the creatures, great and small, scurrying around that woodlot? Were we not inhabitants of a shared space? Clearly my geographic compass was on the fritz. So I returned to the regularizing body of the municipal bylaw once again.

The bylaw helpfully lists approximately two dozen protected species in these woodland groves, but, again, to the exclusion of the buckthorn. As the scientific credo goes, absence of evidence is not evidence of absence and there was only one possible conclusion. The buckthorn was, at the very least, not worthy of protection. It was behaving like a bully in the playground, the kind that steals your beloved Snoopy doll right out of your hands and then rolls it in the mud before handing it back to you, a stunned six-year-old girl, unprepared for such random acts of cruelty. Yes, the buckthorn was the childhood bully manhandling my Snoopy doll in an English school playground. It was a bad seed! It had, as Thomas King says of Christopher Columbus and his rapacious conquistadors, "very bad manners."[8] There was only one kind of plant with such behavioural tendencies: an *invasive* species. The buckthorn had invaded our garden like it had invaded the woodlot. It had leapt over those vegetative walls right into our neighbours'

neighbours' gardens and from our neighbours' neighbours' gardens into our garden with nary a need for sorcery and spells, defiant as all hell. Someone had to fend off the invasion lest it be the death of our garden, much as it was proving to be the certain death of the woodlot.

Ronaldo wasted no time in soldiering up. He got to hacking upper branches, sawing off limbs, putting chainsaws to trunks, uprooting saplings, burning every last twig and tendril he could get his calloused hands on. A massacre ensued but the survival of our garden's biodiversity seemed to depend on it. And we didn't take pleasure in deforesting our back garden, much as we have never taken pleasure in so much as the loss of a single tree, native or non-native. But it was a dirty job and someone had to do it. When every last buckthorn, old and young, had been removed from our garden perimeter, neighbours far and wide might have heard Ronaldo sigh, like the Duke of Wellington on the battlefield, "Believe me, nothing except a battle lost can be half so melancholy as a battle won."

At least in our garden, the European buckthorn, an invasive non-native species par excellence, had met its Waterloo, in Waterloo.

This wise and generous plant, faithfully following the people, became an honored member of the plant community. It's a foreigner, an immigrant, but after five hundred years of living as a good neighbour, people forget that kind of thing.[9]

The Lessons of Tamar-Hind (Fruit of India), or the Gentle Green Giant

Not all non-native trees are so ill-mannered. The buckthorn could take a lesson or two from the tamarind tree of my childhood, or *Tamarindus indica*. As historical records indicate, Arab traders passing through the Indian subcontinent named the fruit tree "Tamar-Hind," meaning the "date fruit of Hind" (aka India), because the fruit's fleshy texture and russet-brown hue resemble those of the date. To most of us in Pakistan and many parts of the Indian subcontinent, tamarind is simply called imli.

Tamarind trees are not retreating creatures. They are twenty-five to thirty metres high, their trunks have a girth of up to eight metres and an expansive crown of branches reaches at least double that girth. In warm, even arid climes, where it thrives, the tree is rarely without foliage but receives a fresh growth with the onset of monsoon season.[10] You might say that the leaves, unlike the tree's impressive stature, are like shrinking violets: they stay open in the sunlight and fold up come sunset. The leaves themselves are classified as pinnate: that is, they hold a perfectly symmetrical series of leaflet pairs on long stems, which produces a light, feathery quality to the tree's otherwise forbidding stature.

When newly settled in Waterloo, I shrieked with delight at the sight of what I mistook for a tamarind tree, incredulous that such a heat-loving specimen would manage to survive here. Of course, this was a classic case of geographical schizophrenia, an act of looking at *the land that is* through the filter of *the land that was*. At any rate, the tree turned out to be a honey locust, native to the southern limits of southern Ontario. The honey locust (not to be confused with the black locust, considered an invasive species in Ontario) also has pinnate compound leaves that are spitting images of the tamarind, and produces fruit in the form of long twisted brown pods that dangle like earrings, or snakes, depending on your perspective, along the tree's upper branches. The gel contained in the pods is consumable by humans, but seems more palatable to the droves of cattle, squirrels and deer that come to feast on its gelatinous offerings – that is, if they can get past the crown of thorns surrounding the trunk and lining the twigs like medieval armour. I recall seeking shade under a honey locust at Ontario's Royal Botanical Gardens' Arboretum, much as I would a tamarind tree in the flagellate sun of the tropics, but I was unceremoniously poked by a large cluster of fallen thorns concealed under overgrown grass at the base of the tree.

I was not entirely wrong to mistake the honey locust for a tamarind, because they hail from the same family: the pea family, or Fabaceae, which includes such a broad range of plants as lupines and wisteria. But the tamarind tree and the fruit it provides are almost synonymous with the Indian subcontinent. Not only is this fruit enjoyed by industrious kids who might be found knocking the ripened pods off the tree with a dunda (a stick), but it is also a staple in South Asian cuisine. Try serving up a plate of samosas without tamarind chutney and you'll have an angry brigade of home-cooks wagging their turmeric-stained fingers at you! It is sold as a densely packed brick, which, when soaked in a tub of hot water, releases the flesh from the seeds, before it is blended with garam masala, red chili, salt and sugar, or used to brighten meat and fish dishes with its tartness. My siblings and I often snuck into the kitchen pantry to chisel away at this tamarind brick with our sticky fingers, dousing it with a ton of salt and then revelling in the contorted facial expressions that came with every mouth-puckering bite! And I can just hear Mum now, admonishing us for using up her secret culinary agents and scaring us with all manner of myths, including the wildly inappropriate warning to my brother that it would turn his voice *girlish*! Even though she may have been right to ward us away from the fruit when we were coming down with a cold – it has been known to aggravate a sore throat – just about every part of the tree, from bark to leaf, holds medicinal salves against anything from constipation to excessive menstruation.

Imagine my delight when the "regular" grocery stores in Waterloo started stocking fresh tamarind. They are packed and exported from Vietnam or Thailand in paper boxes with little plastic windows exposing the unshelled pods, all for a bargain price of $3.99. I have even been accosted by shoppers dawdling in the "exotic" fruits aisle, curious about imported oddities that have as yet to be appropriated by the Gordon Ramsays or Jamie Olivers of this world, and I am always happy to oblige with an explanation.

Oh, that's the tamarind! It's a fruit from South Asia – I mean, India! (I have learned that geographic designations like South Asia don't hold as much currency as India itself, land of the Beatles' and Julia Roberts's [via Elizabeth Gilbert's] spiritual awakening and, of course, the location of the Best Exotic Marigold Hotel.) *You see, you just have to pinch the exterior between your thumb and forefinger till it cracks. Then you scoop out the fleshy pulp inside, being careful not to swallow the seed because each pod consists of segments, kind of like a pea pod, containing a hard, glossy seed.*

Then the difficult but logical question ensues: *But what does it taste like?*

Hmmm. I try, unsuccessfully, to conjure analogies that might resonate with Western palates. *It's pretty unique but you could say it's tangy-sweet.*

Like a blackberry? I see I've failed.

No, more like a . . . like a . . . The customer's partner, standing by the Chiquita bananas, is waving her over, wondering why she's talking to a random stranger hovering by the pitayas, knobbly bitter melon gourds and other alien fruits and vegetables. I try another tack as if I've become an Arab trader of the seventh century pedalling exotic fruits to his desert-dwelling clientele. *Did you know tamarind means "fruit of India"?*

Oh, that's nice.

It's clear I've lost my audience, who walks over to the frowning man by the banana mountain.

See, it's right there in the name – everything you want to know about the tamarind. I'm talking to myself now. I can't think of another fruit named after its place of origin. Writers have even looked to the tamarind as a metonym for the homeland, like Anita Rau Badami's debut novel, *Tamarind Mem*. This is all playing out in my mind as I throw a tamarind box into my shopping cart, thinking it's well worth the $3.99 price of admission.

If its provenance is in the name, surely it is as native a species as they come. Isn't it?

Tamarind may very well have been in the region for hundreds, maybe even thousands of years, but is it a native species or a naturalized species? The jury's still out on this one. Apparently, there is mention of the tamarind in Brahmanic scripture, but perhaps even Brahma can't lay claim to this travelling fruit tree's provenance.[11] Like the apple in Europe, it may have come from elsewhere, felt at home in a compatible climate and eventually became naturalized to just about every partitioned corner of the Indian subcontinent. But its ancient origins – well, that's another story that some claim might take one farther west of the Indian Ocean – to Central or Eastern Africa. The Ethiopians, who were in close contact with the peoples of the Indian subcontinent long before the Arabs, call the pulp of the tamarind *tommar*, which sounds suspiciously like *tamar*,[12] doesn't it? So in which direction did the tamarind first travel, from the Red Sea to the Indian Ocean, or from the Indian Ocean to the Red Sea?

Those little brown pods contain a world of history, I muse, as I pay for my groceries at checkout. As the Mexican brand Jarritos reveals, in its popular tamarind-flavoured soda, Latin Americans have developed a taste for the fruit as well. They turn it into candied balls laced with chili, just like Asians do, from Pakistan to China. After all, the tamarind travelled from the Philippines to Mexico on Spanish imperial galleons, another global trade route that fundamentally altered both the culinary and botanical makeup of the world. In Latin America the tamarind tree has become a naturalized specimen, so much so that no one seems aware of its Asian roots, much as South Asians are largely unaware of what could very well be its African lineage. And speaking of tamarind-soda-guzzling Latinos, I think I fell instantly in love with Ronaldo when I first visited his apartment, because right there, sitting by a south-facing window in the dead of winter, was a baby tamarind tree he had nurtured from seed! Let's call it love at first sight of a slightly different variety. Sometimes, even immigrants from the most wildly distant lands, like Guatemala and Pakistan, find home in each others' gardens!

Like the Arab traders who named it the fruit of India, and the British who renamed it *Tamarindus indica*, we may all have been hoodwinked by the tamarind tree but in the nicest way possible. The tree has played the ultimate botanical trick, making us think that just because it has seemingly *always been here*, it is native to a place. This is because, unlike so many non-native species, the tamarind has not proven to be an invasive species. In fact, the great tamarind tree has proven to be a very neighbourly, hospitable tree, like a gentle green giant. As expansive as it is, botanists praise the tamarind's "symbiotic relationship with certain soil bacteria,"[13] which in turn provides sustenance in the form of nitrogen to other plants growing in its vicinity.

The humble tamarind has succeeded where most humans have failed: it has arrived in many far-flung lands across the globe as a migrant transplant, but it has found a way to live in harmony with its native counterparts. It has somehow managed not to cross that fine line between a non-native species and an invasive species. My beloved imli, tamar-hind, tamarind, tamarindo – call it what you will – deserves our recognition not only as a good-natured transplant but also, perhaps, as a model botanical citizen.

Immigrants cannot by definition be Indigenous to place, but I'm stumbling on the words. Indigenous is a birth-right word. No amount of time or caring changes history or substitutes for soul-deep fusion with the land . . . But if people do not feel "Indigenous," can they nevertheless enter into the deep reciprocity that renews the world?[14]

No Soil Is an Island

I return to our garden with the lessons derived from the tamarind of the past and the buckthorn of the present – or rather the ghost of the buckthorn in the wake of Ronaldo's victory. To be non-native is not, in and of itself, a mark of bad manners. To be a particular kind of non-native species is. This means I don't have to raze the entire garden and start afresh, sourcing only native plants. For one, I imagine there are just as many tamarind-esque plants, naturalized to such a degree that they now behave like native plants, as there are buckthorns, invasive to the point of putting other species at risk. The best I can do is remain alert to the latter (because, let's face it, the buckthorn is here to stay so long as it is in the woodlots or our neighbours' gardens), while protecting the former.

At the same time, I can rectify the glaring absence of native species in our garden. I will do my due diligence and cross-reference my sources, weeding out the imposters (invasive non-natives). I will – and this is a really tough one for self-confessed plant-aholics – resist the urge to buy something because I don't have it, or because it looks pretty, or *just* because it reminds me of other places. I may also have to make an extra effort and drive the distance to nurseries specializing in native species. I may not always come away with the Indigenous names for plants, not only given imperialist naming practices but also given the diversity of Indigenous language communities, each of which might have different names for plants commonly found across Ontario. However, I expect I will come away with a deeper knowledge of the plants that grew here prior to colonization and European settlement, and the significant knowledge they carry regarding land, ecology, food, medicine, culture. Or perhaps I can simply enjoy them for their beauty and the good health they restore to the garden, attracting native pollinators and keeping the garden in flower without the need for "miracle-growing" liquid feeds and pellets.

Like our newly cleared bed that sings with possibility, I will

Garden Inventories

also have to spring-clean our garden vocabulary of all sorts of misnomers that muddy our thinking about what constitutes good- and bad-natured plants. Wildflowers will henceforth simply be thought of as flowers that may or may not be native to the area. If I am to take heed of how deeply intertwined are the worlds of racial and botanical nomenclature, I will notice that wildflowers have been banished from our gardens or, conversely, praised for their undomesticated attributes in much the same way racialized peoples are either ostracized or exoticized for their otherness. In the same vein, I will have to remind myself that weeds are just plants that have similarly suffered the degradation of misrepresentation. Weeds will henceforth be carefully scrutinized for their individual, rather than wholesale, behaviour. If weeds behave badly perhaps there is a method to their madness. Perhaps we might think of weeds as the messenger-plant, alerting us to such things as poor soil quality or even to North American landscaping practices that insist on designing garden beds like sterile industrial sites, with sparsely planted duplicates over large swathes of mulched terrain. Gravity dictates that the millions of seeds dispersed through the air have to land somewhere and who can blame them for thinking that all that exposed earth is an ideal place to germinate?

Which brings me to the question of the land itself. The soil in our garden is clearly not the same as the soil in that woodlot or any other natural habitat. It has been turned, churned and likely also burned by chemicals and pesticides in ways that have made it unrecognizable to native species. Similarly, the soil in the woodlot, surrounded by hectares of urban development and industry, is likely not the same as the soil in other forests better shielded from urbanity's tentacles. At least here, in the city of Waterloo, both woodlot and garden are also downwind from the province's largest stretch of agricultural land. All those fields of corn and soya may look uniformly self-contained but their porous borders are easily breached by the particulate matter of pesticides and other foreign agents. And if seeing is believing such airborne connections between garden and agri-farm, last summer we actually found a wheat stalk sprouting in our garden. No soil is an island. As Caribbean poet Jean "Binta" Breeze might say, beneath every island summit there lies an ocean, under which "we hold hands."[15]

From Ten Thousand Steps to Meta-Forays

The garden is singing with possibility now. Light streams through the dappled willow and American horse chestnut. The back bed is a blank canvas. The rose has been carefully transplanted by Ronaldo who feels it still has a place here, though not quite as prominent a place as it once enjoyed. And even I, with my inherited antipathy to roses, am as delighted by its delicate pink bouquets as I am impressed by its ability to flower well into October, alongside some of its hardier native counterparts, like oginiig. Ronaldo did well to ignore my protests against this rambling rose specimen, which has given new meaning to one of my favourite acrylic paint pigments: permanent rose. The garden seems equally content to share its space with this permanent settler.

I return to my list-making inspired by the creeks and woodlots, and even the river trail at the foot of our neighbourhood, putting a check mark by all the shrubs that portend to be good neighbours out there and here in the garden. They include:

- Juneberry
- ninebark
- highbush cranberry
- elderberry

Garden Inventories

- yellow twig dogwood
- nannyberry (*Viburnum lentago*)
- staghorn sumac

During one of our autumnal walks, I notice the city has pruned the red osier dogwoods to near oblivion, and I feel compelled to salvage a tangle of limbs in the aftermath of this municipal massacre. We carry the wounded along the five-thousand-step-return journey home, where we immediately insert them into the newly cleared, anti-buckthorn back bed, imagining the much-needed infusion of colour they will provide in the winter, when their scarlet branches stand out against a backdrop of stark-white snow. As if this is not gift enough, autumn yields other native treasures around the creek:

- purple aster
- goldenrod (which I am slowly discovering is, like the aster, replete with variety)
- cup plant
- grey-headed coneflower
- Joe-pye weed
- pale jewelweed

Careful not to uproot them, we collect a handful of seeds and scatter them in the garden. I take my cue from Ronaldo, who carries his own Indigenous knowledge with him, from Central to North America. He's always had the good instinct to harvest seeds, unlike my own consumer-driven tendencies that drive me to nurseries for the instant gratification to be found in mass-propagated ornamentals.

Garden Inventories

Luckily, the creek is a seed-harvester's paradise, the milkweeds proving to be particularly irresistible. Their freshly opened pods bursting with seeds nestled in beds of tufted hair makes me crave a

favourite childhood treat known as "buddhi ki baal" or "old lady's hair" – a sweet street food in South Asia. I catch my reflection in the black creek water, a woman with a few milkweed tufts of her own aging hair. She is on a mission with sandwich bags and a pair of secateurs (one never knows when a shrubby branch might offer itself as a potential cutting), and when she catches her reflection again, she sees her mother staring back at her. Our seamless metamorphosis into our parents tends to jump out at us in such moments, but I am pleased by this development, even honoured to continue my mother's work in this way – to bear her spirit in these activities. I channel her every time Ronaldo and I take a road trip, and I am on the verge of either shouting, "Stop the car!" or hitting the brakes myself, to harvest a few seeds from a field of lupines, or to take a closer look at a plant spotted from the window of a speeding car with Mum's eagle-like vision.

It is also Robin Wall Kimmerer, botanist and member of the Citizen Potawatomi Nation, I think of now. Her book *Braiding Sweetgrass: Indigenous Wisdom, Scientific Knowledge, and the Teachings of Plants* has been another kind of spirit guide through these nature walks. I think specifically of the chapter titled "Asters and

Garden Inventories

Goldenrod" as we harvest a variety of asters (I count at least three: calico, New England and large-leaved aster), shaking their tiny seeds into used sandwich bags, to be stored later in larger paper bags saved up from the liquor store. Together, the asters and goldenrods make for a painterly display of purple and gold (oddly, the mascot colours of the university that employs me) in the sunniest, meadow-like part of the creek. Their tendency to flower well into late fall is a winning feature that less hardy non-native species are ill-equipped to provide. In the fifteen years of walking along this creek I have noticed the asters and goldenrods appear, each September, as companion flowers, along with the spiky-headed teasels whose seeds the birds can't get enough of, so we leave them be. Kimmerer calls this "September pairing of purple and gold" a form of "lived reciprocity." For her, such harmonizing opens us up to other kinds of reciprocal thinking, which require a small but significant leap from the literal to the figurative. She calls this type of thinking *metaphoray*, a play on the words *metaphor* and *foray* (the type of forays botanists take for field research). She describes *metaphoray* as the power to walk through and imagine one's world with all of one's senses: "mind, body, emotion, and spirit." Understood this way, the asters and goldenrods offer up their secrets as complementary beings. They invite us to take a leap into figurative thinking, one in which "Indigenous knowledge and Western science"[16] might also dance like

asters and goldenrods, not in states of ideological antagonism, but in warm, neighbourly, organic reciprocity.

At the end of a good long day of gardening, then, I hope to arrive at a place where the conservation areas and wild habitats of *out there* and the garden of *in here* are not so diametrically opposed – where they might enter metaphoray and achieve new forms of reciprocal thinking. The seeds, like the garden, are our own experiment in metaphoray, and sometimes we will get it right and sometimes we will fail. But this time round, the garden will not be a place we hope to slavishly mould and reimagine in the rear-view mirror of an émigré's nostalgia. And perhaps it will tell a story of this place and a story of us, in this place, extending the power of reciprocity even further, to include Indigenous, Western and even non-Western knowledge. It will remind us that even though we are not Indigenous to this land, this does not mean we have to reconcile ourselves to an imposter-status. Non-native we may be, but invasive we can choose *not* to be.

Our plant list grows in the awareness that our garden, like the creeks and woodlots, will always be in a state of flux, continuously transformed by its surrounding environment and our own botanical interventions. If those walks around the creeks and woodlots have taught me anything it is that flora doesn't recognize borders.

Garden Inventories

If our garden has taught me anything it is that it doesn't look to a fossilized past, it looks to the present and the future.

After ten thousand steps and counting, Mountain Man and I look forward to all the ground we have as yet to cover, in these, our shared garden inventories.

Garden Postscript

How much has the garden changed since those pandemic walks! A few years on, this square pocket of land is teeming with so much variety that our garden inventory might require its own illustrated booklet! The flowers – including Canada anemone, purple aster, bergamot, cup plant, blanket flower, hyssop, echinacea, coneflower, blue flax, spotted geranium, black-eyed Susan, goldenrod, rose mallow, campion, rose of Sharon, milkweed, columbine, tickseed, buttercup, evening primrose – have all had time to settle in, providing us a seed bank of our own. Where the buckthorn battle was once waged there now sits a native shrubbery that brings year-round colour and interest, not to mention a variety of berries, including those of the Juneberry, red osier dogwood, ninebark and black lace elderberry. The once hemmed-in hostas, one of which is even named "gentle giant" and bears the tamarind's non-native-but-non-invasive disposition, regale us with silver-blue and chartreuse foliage, as well as elegant flower stalks, almost like a thank-you note for the king-size beds that now better accommodate their generous proportions. As the fruiting mulberry tree matures (still slowly but surely), we are happy enough to share its delectable fruit with visiting fauna; it's the least we can do, since we are so often the recipient of *their* gifts. Those gifts that do not threaten our little ecosystem we receive with pleasure, including a white elm . . . or could it be that rare species of "rock elm" highlighted in the Eastbridge Woodlot interpretive sign? And even though this year saw the end of our dwindling Jack pines (mainly to old age and some nasty winter storms), Ronaldo's eastern white pines appreciate their moment in the sun on our front lawn. Though every time I imagine the white pines in their natural habitat – not the circumscribed woodlots but the immense forests of this land – I feel they must be missing some of their favourite companions, like white birch and red oak.

I return to the inventory – this time, taking note of future plantings. Whether or not we have room in the garden is a matter to be discussed and debated with Ronaldo, preferably out on the patio over a mug of chai or a glass of wine:

- white (or paper) birch
- red oak
- silver maple (because how can we have a Canadian garden without a *Canadian* maple?)
- a native fruit tree is a must. But what?

The last item on my aspirational list sends me back into research mode and I am immediately drawn to a small native fruiting tree called the pawpaw. The pawpaw is native to the Carolinian life zone and considered one of Canada's rarest species, at risk thanks to the usual suspects like colonization, agriculture and urbanization. Fortunately, conservation efforts by ecologists hoping to regenerate and restore Ontario's biodiversity, as well as historians who recognize in the fruit its significance to Indigenous peoples, seem hopeful. I have to confess that my interest in the pawpaw is quite personal, as the fruit is often described as having a distinctly "tropical" profile and flavour. In fact, the pawpaw belongs to the Annonaceae, or custard-apple family, and Ronaldo and I both grew up eating a variety of custard apple in Guatemala (where it is known as annona) and Pakistan (where it is known as sharifa).[17]

Who would disagree that a fruiting tree that is native to southern Ontario *and* part of a larger tropical fruit family is the perfect addition to our garden inventory, almost like a natural bridge between *the land that is, the lands that were* and *the land becoming.*

Startling Lawn Facts

Startling Lawn Fact #1: The grass family, Poaceae,[1] is one of the largest plant families, and one of the most important to humans, as it includes agricultural grains such as wheat, rice, maize (corn) and sugar cane. The sugar in your tea is part of the same plant family as the lawn on which you slide into home base.[2]

Primal moans and guttural cries of "yee-ah" got us out of bed. My brother, sister and I huddled around the big bay window overlooking the Halifax Common in our new pajamas and housecoats. It was June 1987. Our first month in Canada, when everything felt new. From the flannel clothes on our backs, to the arctic tinge in the summer air, to the strange noises waking us up on a Sunday morning.

"Who's making such a racket?" Dad harrumphed while channel surfing for the news.

Garden Inventories

"Out there!" I pointed at a group of men scattered around an expansive green field, amused by how much their striped outfits resembled our pajamas.

Mum peered over us, a piping hot cup of tea in hand. "What's the point of such a big park without a single tree?"

"It's a cricket field," Dad mumbled from the recliner.

"They don't play cricket here, Dad! They play baseball!" My brother and I rolled our eyes with the kind of teenage contempt reserved for parents. It's not as if a group of men tossing around a bat and ball on a perfectly manicured lawn was anything new. In Pakistan, well-worn cricket fields were emblems of national pride. In Karachi, we'd also spent languorous afternoons sipping nimbo pani (freshly squeezed lemonade) and nibbling cucumber sandwiches at gymkhanas, where the manicured lawn was a central feature of the gentlemen's clubs inherited from our former British colonizers.

Perhaps this is where the lawn to which we'd been exposed on this early Sunday morning and the earlier lawns of our childhood parted ways. The Halifax Common was designed as a public and civic-minded space, the gymkhana, as a private and wholly elitist space. After all, who can really afford to maintain a water-hogging lawn in hot climates but the privileged few? Outside the guarded walls of the gymkhana maintained by an army of uniformed staff, the manicured lawn was an imported idea. On this score, we had the British to thank for giving the world yet another calling card of privilege. Because the lawn begins with Lancelot "Capability" Brown and other notable European landscape architects of the eighteenth century. The lawn grew as a symbol of British affluence in what was still a predominantly agricultural economy, making the bold statement that hectares of land, normally the reserve of grazing livestock, could be co-opted and mowed, at great expense, for little more than their aesthetic value.³ Almost as if these pristine plains of green, devised by Brown as the template for the English country estate, were a balm against the ugliness of other kinds of monocrop environments, like the slave plantation system in Britain's overseas colonies, or even as an antidote to the billowing factory smoke and grime of the nation's rising industrial age.

The perfect green lawn, at least for Brown and his clientele, was hardly a common sight for the common man. It was designed precisely for its uncommonness in a land strictly divided between the haves and have-nots. I was reminded of these divisions while binge-watching *Downton Abbey*, the immensely popular British television series filmed at Highclere Castle, an authentic English country estate park designed by Capability Brown in the late 1700s for the first earl of Carnarvon. Even though the story humanizes domestic servants polishing silver and churning butter in dingy manor basements, there is no sign of the external workforce keeping the estate's manor grounds in tip-top shape with scythes and upper body strength. There's a special kind of symmetry in the image of lowly "commoners" swinging the Grim Reaper's blade for the bluebloods' lawns of yesteryear, and the contemporary commoners swinging baseball bats for recreational sport on the public lawns of today.

This is not to say the swarthy English groundskeepers of yesteryear did not also enjoy, as much as their settler-colonial counterparts, a leisurely Sunday afternoon at the Commons. The word *lawn* first appeared in Middle English as *launde*, which translates as a glade or opening in the woods. In medieval times, the launde was used as a common meadow that morphed into a lawn by the time the local villagers' livestock, who were left there to graze, ate to satiation. So, while the British lords and ladies sipped imported Darjeeling tea and played croquet on their immaculate lawns, the village folk likely congregated, gossiped, drank a pint of ale or two and danced at the slightly more rustic village launde. Those who shared rights of usage to such "common" tracts of land were called "commoners."[4]

In the same spirit, King George III granted 235 acres of common land "for the use of the inhabitants of the Town of Halifax forever." Halifax, Nova Scotia, that is. This was 1763, a time when much of this decreed common land came to be used, as it was in Medieval England, for livestock grazing and public gatherings, but notably also for military purposes. Not only did our first apartment in Canada overlook the Halifax Common, Canada's oldest urban park in one of the Dominion's oldest cities, it also sat west of Citadel Hill and a few doors down from the old Halifax Armoury. On the Commons' carefully groomed exterior lay the foundation of Haligonian identity as a military town, and one of the most fortified bases outside Europe. In the old Dominion, then, the Commons was quickly usurped by the army, where it set the stage for military parades and training. And the army also used it as a space of refuge for the masses during a cholera outbreak, and as a shelter for the victims of the Halifax Explosion in December 1917.[5]

Our culture shock that first Sunday morning as new immigrants waking up in our first home stemmed from how seemingly little we had in common with baseball, baseball players and diamond-shaped green spaces. But the desire to recreate a foreign landscape in Britain's image, with its sweeping lawn-green vistas, was something we had already witnessed as former subjects of the British Empire. One way or another, the new chapter in the book of our migrant lives was bound up, as it was for those baseball players, with that perfectly manicured lawn.

Startling Lawn Facts

Startling Lawn Fact #2: As of 2005, a NASA study estimates that lawns covered an estimated 128,000 square kilometres or almost thirty-two million acres of the United States of America. That's about the size of Texas.[6] By now that number has reached forty million acres. Though Canada does not appear to have a corresponding statistic, the Government of Canada devotes a page, under the category "Health" and subcategory "Healthy Living," to "Starting and Caring for a Lawn," suggesting that it occupies as much mental space, if not physical space, as it does in the United States.

My father was quick to find a house, and our front-row seat to the Commons was soon replaced with a view of residential lawns in a suburb called Clayton Park, just up the road from Halifax's Bedford Basin. Our new house was perched on a small hilly cul-de-sac. The houses were all brick, which was a contrast to the city's reliance on vinyl siding, a building material that was new to us and reminded me of the shipping containers lined up at the Halifax port. Another unusual feature of the house, which I didn't much care for at the time, was the woodsy back garden. Mum loved it, or at least she saw its potential, but in its raw greenness I saw the antithesis to the City of Manila, the exhilarating metropolis we had left behind for Canada, the land that Dad had originally set his émigré's sights on. He had travelled to Canada in the 1970s, eager to start his family's immigration process when, according to nuclear-family lore, his mother said she wanted to live in England, and so, being the ever-dutiful son, he shelved those plans to grant his mother's wish.

While Canada was the dream-deferred and dream-realized for Dad, leaving the Philippines was, for me, the dream-smashed-into-a-thousand-and-one-heartbroken-pieces. I was poised for my

Garden Inventories

senior year at the International School Manila, I was in the throes of my first enduring romance and I was part of a sisterhood of friends from all over the world: India, the Philippines, Hong Kong, Holland, South Korea, the United States. I had felt the searing pain of those goodbyes the first moment my father said we were leaving, but I hadn't counted on the pain of letting go of a country I had also come to love, for its pulsating tropical energy and its ability to welcome strangers with none of the snobbery and xenophobia we had faced in England. I felt my teenage rites of passage were being stolen from me: convocation with my own graduating class, continued delinquent adventures with my besties, the bittersweet pain of letting first-love romance run its natural course.

Teenage angst notwithstanding, my adolescent years in the Philippines had already exposed me to enduring experiences for which my adult self is eternally grateful. Our school was a lesson in the global world order, with teachers imported from places like Ohio and Nebraska – white Americans paid twice the salary of our Filipino teachers – and where locals were treated as second-class citizens by an expatriate community, both white and non-white. The Philippines provided a crash course on what it means to be colonized in ways that I was too young to grasp as a child in Pakistan, no doubt setting the stage for my academic career and a lifelong study of the histories and literatures of European imperialism. And, of course, how could we escape the empire in islands colonized by Spain for over three hundred and fifty years (longer than most Latin American countries), and then by the United States for another half-century. Attentive as I am to the power of names, I was struck by Pulitzer Prize–winning journalist Jose Antonio Vargas's description of the cultural schizophrenia created by this history of multiple occupation: "After the Americans forced the Spanish out of the Philippines, their typewriters couldn't type accented vowels. . . . My name is Jose because of Spanish colonialism. But Jose isn't José because of American imperialism."[7]

The Philippines we came to know, from 1983 to 1987, was a sovereign nation, but the signs of neo-imperial occupation were nowhere more apparent than in the massive US naval (Subic Bay) and air force (Clark) bases, each of which covered an area roughly the size of the island nation of Singapore. The Subic Bay naval base was established in 1901 by Theodore Roosevelt, and Subic Bay and Clark were considered the two most important overseas US military installations for close to a century. They were also a permanent reminder that sovereignty is a fiction few outside the western hemisphere actually believe. This fiction assumed a satirical dimension when the United States only saw fit to relinquish control of these sites after the volcanic eruption of nearby Mount Pinatubo (which sits about ninety kilometres northwest of Manila) in 1991. Nature achieved an anti-imperial revolution where human interventions had failed.

The bases were active military facilities during our residency in the Philippines and, oddly enough, they became an extension of our adolescent world in the season of intramural competitive sports. After our school buses passed multiple security checkpoints, we would be allowed to go head to head with the kids of American military personnel. It was easy to figure out that we expat kids were among the privileged few to be granted access to these formidable military encampments. Even my parents would have no such right of access. And certainly not my Filipino boyfriend. Visiting Subic Bay and Clark under the watchful eye of armed soldiers was, for teenagers, like stepping into the set of a Hollywood film. How could reality and fantasy not collide in a place so artfully contrived to resemble small-town USA, every aspect of the base like an elaborate set design with American supermarkets, a theatre, a chamber hall, an American Express National Bank... and, yes, lots and lots of lawn, not only for military drills but also for a golf course, that most American of recreational lawn activities (albeit with Scottish roots). It was on those very same heavily guarded lawns that I participated in my first cross-country competition, a tortuous circuit under the blazing tropical sun, and I was always among the last half-dozen or so kids to cross the finish line, but I didn't care – this, too, was well worth the price of admission.

All this to say that the woodsy Canadian garden was not exactly screaming "home" to me yet. And the front lawn was also doing little to assuage those tropical yearnings. From my front-lawn-facing bedroom window in Clayton Park, I could see everyone's homes and they could see ours but we still didn't know them and they didn't know us. My eight-year-old sister, Nooreen, was the only one to befriend a neighbour's daughter, an important lesson about kids and dogs being bridges to community that I would come to learn the hard way, as a new homeowner in Waterloo, where we had neither kids nor dogs to break the proverbial ice. Sometimes a kid could be spotted pedalling around a driveway like a guppy in a fishbowl but, in a cold climate, playtime transpired indoors or in the inner sanctum of the backyard, which seemed as restricted an area as Subic Bay and Clark.

The manicured, treeless facade of the front lawn, like the dense thicket of woods that constituted the back garden, were spaces I felt unready to occupy. It took a dog, our first and only Canadian pet, to teach me something about our new environment when he hightailed it after a squirrel. Floyd was a rambunctious part beagle, part German shepherd. My brother and I named him after Pink Floyd, a band that arguably captured some of the disaffection we had as yet to shake off, like an electrified 1980s' perm. Floyd, whose pedigree was as muddled as our own, bore none of our

Startling Lawn Facts

self-consciousness, taking full ownership of Clayton Park, which he forced us to conquer like David Livingstones standing perilously close to Victoria Falls. When Floyd wriggled his way off his leash, he would run unobstructed, from one front lawn to the next. As I watched him bound across the neighbours' properties, I realized that quite unlike the Filipino neighbourhoods we had left behind, this suburban street had neither gate nor fence nor hedge – nothing to demarcate one house from the next. For a girl raised on Islamic principles, there was something vulgar about all this unabashed openness, as if the houses pranced about in shameless exhibitionism. Naked and exposed, it was no wonder each homeowner defended their turf with lawn signs like *Pesticide Application: Keep Off!* or *Lawn Care in Progress: Do Not Enter!* I got the message loud and clear but Floyd was blissfully illiterate so the burden fell on our shoulders to keep him off *everyone's grass*.

The expanse of green space certainly looked like a "common" area in suburbia, and it was even governed by unwritten codes of social conduct: namely, that the grass be shorn to a predetermined length of 1.5 inches, like the sailors' crewcuts from the Subic Bay naval base or the ones on shore leave down at the Halifax Harbour. And like all systems of governance, adherence to this unwritten code established a civic solidarity – a unified front against Mother Nature. It was as if each of these two diametrically opposed garden landscapes – the barren front lawn, devoid of vegetation and signs of life, and the wooded back garden, inhospitable and foreboding – were symbols of the duality that was our new alien Canadian landscape: the first of nature's abject defeat against human intervention, and the other of nature's shaking fist, a wilderness that refused to submit. We had arrived on a battlefield where the neighbours formed a united front, all of them foot soldiers in a culture of lawn maintenance to which we had better adapt lest we found ourselves banished like the dandelions daring to rear their yellow heads amid a sea of neutered green. Lest we found ourselves branded undesirables, like the lowly weeds. Lest we found ourselves uprooted. Again.

Startling Lawn Fact #3: By continually keeping our lawns mowed to the prescribed 1.5 inches, lawn grass is like a neutered pet, a sterile creature never afforded the dignity of going to seed but also kept alive in its neutered state. Environmental journalist Michael Pollan refers to lawns as "nature purged of sex and death," given the lawn's perverse state of being kept alive but not long enough to reproduce.[8]

It stood to reason that the construct of the lawn had travelled to the Americas with the people of the British Isles. But, as our own lives as denizens confirmed, social and cultural constructs, like people, undergo all kinds of mutations in the process of migration. Authors Virginia Scott Jenkins and Ted Steinberg agree, in two popular studies of lawn culture, that the lawn not only grew as an idea in the climates and topographies of North America, but mutated into a full-blown "obsession" therein.

Lawn culture wasn't an overnight success story. In fact, lawn grass, or what eventually became lawn grass after decades of scientific and commercial tampering, is itself another kind of immigrant. Prior to colonization native grasses mainly appeared in the prairies, savannahs and steppes of North America. As David Suzuki tells us in a *Nature of Things* episode featuring the Canadian Prairies, once settlers arrived, these native grasses were decimated by newly introduced livestock, and farmers quickly turned to imported grass to reproduce meadows and pastures otherwise alien to the North American environment.⁹ Other kinds of grasses arrived inadvertently, including by way of the Transatlantic slave trade, so that guinea grass and Bermuda grass from the African continent became nativized even before mass European settlement. It also stood to reason that not all types of grass were suitable for the highly varied climates of North America, from the subtropical to the subarctic. If you've ever wondered why grass seed sold at Canadian Tire and Home Depot bear the label Pro-Mix, it is because they contain a grab bag of non-native grasses, including ryegrass, tall fescue and Canada bluegrass, best adapted to cooler environments.

In Canada and the United States, the common term *yard* suggests that well into the twentieth century a garden was little more than an enclosed space of packed dirt surrounding a building. The yard served a number of important functions: an open-air shed for tools and household items, a dumping ground for trash and, for some, a space for growing vegetables or other subsistence produce. Anyone coming from a warmer climate will tell you that grasses, especially taller grasses, can harbour insects, rodents or, horror of horror, snakes, so lawns weren't immediately embraced as an idea in the southern states, either. In the Philippines, we lived in a subdivision on the outskirts of Manila called Valle Verde (Green Valley). In the relatively modest environs of Valle Verde – unlike other gated communities reserved for expats receiving generous "hazard-pay" salaries for the hardship of living like royalty in the perilous "Third World" – gardens consisted of short strips of land at the front, side and back of the house. One side was reserved as the spot where live-in maids, a common feature in all middle-to-upper-class households, could do household chores, the remaining spaces used for landscaping of some sort. Grass, at least in these smaller lots, was a rarity and used sparsely. One day there was pandemonium on our street because someone had spotted a venomous snake living the life of the reptilian one percent in an empty lot that had gone to bush just a few doors down. The brave soul who caught and most likely killed the snake certainly did not receive any hazard pay. To this day, I shudder at the thought of high grasses in the tropics, and can only imagine the terrors slithering around the sandalled feet of plantation workers who still have to venture out into other kinds of grasslands, like sugar cane fields and rice paddies.

Back in the colonies of North America, the lawn was an elitist construct well into the nineteenth century. I came across this phenomenon in another TV drama, *The Gilded Age*, also by *Downton Abbey* creator Julian Fellowes. The series follows the lives of New York's old-moneyed gentry duking it out with the nouveau riche as the latter amass enough wealth to break the former's vaulted glass ceilings. I encourage you to watch the show, if only to notice the little green patch of lawn fronting the Russells' (a fictional family likely modelled after the Vanderbilts) palatial home. This patch of lawn, a miniature replica of landscape architect André Le Nôtre's *tapis vert* or "green carpet" motif found throughout the grounds of the Palace of Versailles, exhibits the Russells' penchant for the garish tastes of the French aristocracy, which they are seen to impose on this democratized "New World" setting. But as history bears out, it is the Russells, and not their social gatekeepers, who would set the tone for the next century. Like their ostentatious house, that patch of lawn was an act of rebellion against prevailing norms that would transform the tastes and habits of future landowning North Americans. When the elite of North America started to emulate their European counterparts (English and French alike), so did "the new aesthetic of the front lawn."[10] The front lawn aesthetic took time to trickle down to the Everyman by way of such things as town beautification projects and garden clubs but eventually the *tapis vert* took hold as a very American idea, in the front yards and backyards of the working middle class.

By the twentieth century, lawn cultivation was not an organic process so much as a wholesale adoption by design, advanced by figures such as Frederick Law Olmsted, the first to create a blueprint for iconic American parks like Central Park in Manhattan, as well as American suburbia. The two elements – park and suburbia – were merged to mimic the park-like settings of the elite (remember Capability Brown's estate lawns). As the name of our old Halifax suburb Clayton Park suggests, such communities were intended to appear park-like in setting and character – at least park-like in the way it was framed by Olmsted and other American landscape architects. The seamless lawns of our Haligonian cul-de-sac were starting to make sense, but it was only upon a visit to an acquaintance's house in the United States that I fell witness to one of the most absurd instances of this suburban trope. This house sat among a street of similarly supersized McMansions, each one boasting about an acre or more of flat land. Or at least I had the impression of acreage because each lawn ran freely into the next, without so much as a tree, shrub or fence setting one property apart from the next. If this was to emulate a park-like setting, it was the most barren and characterless park I had ever seen. Floyd would have liked it though.

Ferris Jabr, of *Scientific American*, notes that with the first mass-produced suburban community, the front lawn took hold as the pre-eminent landscape template for gardens across the United States.[11] This wholesale adoption of the lawn was aided and abetted by the increasing affordability of lawn mowers, by commercially packaged carcinogenic chemical warfare against undesirables like the dandelion, by scientific research devoted to grass cultivation and by an increasingly wealthy postwar generation. We can see how the suburban model is reproduced across North America, from Thunder Bay, Canada, to Brownsville, USA. There are even scrappy patches of grass clinging on for dear life like a balding man's comb-over in the glacial landscapes of Iqaluit, Canada's northernmost city, and I bet you ten US dollars the same is true for Utqiagvik, Alaska. In southern Ontario, land is at such a premium that few can afford the model suburban home set back a good nine metres from the road where the lawn assumes its rightful place in the sun. However, one need only look at today's shrinking properties, where postage-stamp front yards are no bigger than the one square metre of turf covering them, to see just how attached North Americans are, on both sides of the border, to the lawn as a sociocultural and, perhaps, socioeconomic ideal.

But here's the paradox (or maybe more than one paradox in this class-addled society): a capitalist culture obsessed with individualism and the right to private property has adopted a residential model of unrelenting conformity and the illusion of communalism. Even fifty years hence, if one blade of grass on a homeowner's lawn were to grow above the prescribed 1.5 inches, the whole collective ecosystem would be thrown into anarchic disgrace.

Startling Lawn Fact #4: Between 1947 and 1951, Abe Levitt and his sons built a network of homes on the potato fields of Long Island, along with 17,544 new lawns. Levittown emerged as the prototype of American suburbia that endures well into the twenty-first century. Levitt was passionate about lawns, and is known to have said, "No man who owns his own house and lot can be a communist. . . . He has too much to do."[12]

Startling Lawn Facts

Our Waterloo neighbourhood is part of a subdivision called Colonial Acres, developed in the 1960s by Charles Voelker, who seemed smitten with the park-like settings and model colonial homes of American suburbia. Colonial Acres is further subdivided into its older and newer wings. Our wing has approximately one hundred homes, of which about half a dozen or fewer are without a front lawn. This means less than 10 percent have rejected the front lawn construct in preference for a more natural landscape that includes some combination of trees, natural ground cover, flowers and shrubs (xeriscaping hasn't caught on in a country that holds one of the planet's greatest renewable supplies of fresh water). Even fewer homes have any sort of barrier, natural or fabricated, and those that do boldly stand out from the pack. The rest are not without vegetation but landscaping is designed so as not to obfuscate the homes from street-view. Many of the homes occupied by some of the earliest residents, where one would imagine a profusion of mature trees and shrubs, have the most spartan front lawns. Our front lawn sits somewhere between these approaches. When we were house hunting, the property really stood out on account of the little copse of Jack pines that gave the house a treed and private facade. I must confess that I loved the combination of trees and lawn, because it must have sparked my own childhood memories of Britain's national parks. I also liked this property's (*backyard*) six-foot fence in a neighbourhood where only those with swimming pools or rambunctious dogs like Floyd build fences. And we have neither pool nor dog here.

One rarely sees the front lawn put to any use in Colonial Acres, much like the Clayton Park of our North American suburban initiation. Human activity on these street-facing squares of green only consists of lawn maintenance, from raking off the eerie white film (snow mould), which appears after six months of winter, to lawn aeration, mowing, savage tousles with dandelions, setting up sprinkler systems, fertilizing, reseeding and sometimes resodding – and, for some, the singular obsession of leaf blowing. One summer I tried a little experiment by setting up a deck chair and table on my front lawn to capitalize on the shade of the Jack pines. Secretly, I was also hoping to make a statement in the dissident spirit of our lawn-free neighbours. In my case, the manifesto would read: *Front lawns can be useful places, too!* I spent a few afternoons reading books, or pretending to, before I grew more than a bit self-conscious out there where even the neighbour's dog, tied to a post on the front lawn directly across from ours, seemed agitated by my presence.

Curiously, one does not quite appreciate the full magnitude of lawn-worship in North America till the fall season. In a country emblematized by the maple leaf it is startling to see how furiously these national symbols are raked up, blown to oblivion, bagged and disposed of, by homeowner and municipality alike. I would hazard to say that people who grow up in two-season climates (hot-and-dry and hot-and-wet) silently nurse a bad case of autumn envy. When two-season people head to four-season climates, we expect nothing less than an autumnal spectacle. We expect to see those leaves whipped up by an arctic wind; we want to feel the crunch of fallen leaves underfoot; we want the full blushing Virginia creeper and Boston ivy league experience, damn it! Alas, little did I know that suburbia would rob us of this dream, where leaf blowers generate maple leaf tornadoes that eventually settle, in energy-depleted rain-soaked leaf mounds, at the edge of sidewalks for municipal "curbside leaf collection." But nobody really wins this frenzied rush to clear away the leaves. Squirrels and birds are denied their nesting material, frogs and insects their winter canopy, and even the lawns are deprived of the precious nutrients decomposing leaves would have provided.

Startling Lawn Facts

All this toil and trouble for a perfect lawn in a country where that lawn is buried under several feet of snow for a good six months of the year makes me think of Levitt's point about communists and lawns. He's right about the kind of busywork lawn maintenance entails. No one can afford clandestine meetings at the local socialist chapter when Saturday lawn maintenance and Sunday mass devour most of the weekend! But surely all that aesthetic, cultural, social and environmental sameness betrays a level of conformity that runs counter to the rights, freedoms and privileges so cherished by the democratic state.

Ah, but there's that word again – *privilege* – mucking things up like a maple tree's autumn cascade. What appears to be the democratization of space and landownership turns out to be, like the fictional Russells' miniature Palace of Versailles, aspirational elitism. Hear ye, settler colonials and neo-colonials of America, come shed the yoke of your feudal ancestors in the garden of *their* classist dreams.

Startling Lawn Fact #5: Lawn is the most grown crop in the United States, and it's not a crop anyone can eat – not even our resident wildlife, who would and likely do perish from the more lethal fertilizers and pesticides used on the lawn. This makes the lawn the costliest crop in North America, consuming the equivalent of nine billion gallons of water per day to keep green. That's two hundred gallons of potable water per person per day.

In 2025, Ronaldo and I will celebrate our twenty-fifth wedding anniversary, though I'm proud to say we've already reached the

Garden Inventories

quarter-century milestone, having met in 1997. We got married on August fifth because the civil court in Montreal was all booked up on the seventh, which was our preference. One might say the number five has come to bear symbolic weight in our lives.

In my case, I have lived in twenty-three homes, which numerically adds up to five. My mother, with a penchant for the supernatural, often remarked that the number five followed us from continent to continent; many of our homes bore some variation of five in their address: 23, 32, 14 and so on. When I first met Ronaldo and told him this curious tidbit about our lives, he informed me, with a level of genuine concern I found utterly endearing, that the number five, in Mayan astronomy, is considered the *unluckiest* number. In the Mayan calendar, the *wayeb* refers to the five "nameless" days in the year when the earth was unprotected by the gods. Now as such beliefs would dictate, it was in our Manila house, which bore the number 23, where my father spent most of his time trying to recuperate a substantial business investment lost to a Pakistani con man, and then to a judicial system choreographed by corrupt officials. Now that I think back to this tumultuous episode in our lives, it is not the financial hit my father suffered that saddens me so much as the emotional price of having fallen prey to false expressions of brotherhood in a foreign and friendless land. Alas, living in a house numbered 23 did not serve us well in Manila, but it carried its biggest blow in a Montreal apartment numbered 14, because this is the home in which my mother contracted a viral infection, fifteen years before Covid was a household word, that took her life in a matter of a week. The sting of family history must have cast a long shadow, because we're still on the alert for inauspicious street addresses.

And yet here we are, on the eve of our *twenty-third* wedding anniversary, united in our defiance against both familial and cosmic numerological doom! Ronaldo mans the lamb chops sizzling on the barbecue as I prep a dish of hummus and uncork a bottle of wine. Charred flesh wafts from the barbecue, no doubt setting the neighbourhood dogs' olfactory glands ablaze, as I wax poetic about the benefits of lamb in a beef-obsessed culture. In fact, even in the farmland surrounding the Waterloo region, it is unusual to see sheep pastures, much of the lamb consumed here still of the imported variety and likely raised on a diet of fresh New Zealand grasses, guaranteed to be antibiotic-free, hormone-free and stress-free, from pasture to plate.

I pour out two glasses of wine as the cardinals begin their nightly serenade, a scarlet male courting his brown-backed lady love with a song we have anthropomorphized as "Hi, Sweetie! Hi, Sweetie!" The garden is bursting with life and colour, which calls for a celebratory toast, when a mechanical noise, like a motorcycle in full throttle, sends the birds into amber alert as they seek camouflage in the bushes.

I try to savour my glass of wine, its earthy minerality summarily doused by a distant lawn mower's gasoline emissions. "Wouldn't you know it! Just as soon as we sit down to dinner!"

"Like clockwork." Ronaldo glances at his Fitbit, as another lawn mower powers up, and then another, and another.

"I guess ours is a bit overgrown, too," Ronaldo says.

"What? I can't hear you!"

"I said, maybe I should mow the lawn tonight!"

"Have mercy!" I scoff down my lamb chop and retreat indoors to save my hearing and sanity from the lawn mowers and, at least in one front yard, a leaf blower set to maximum one hundred CFM (the maximum rate of air pressure expelled in cubic feet per minute). Once 9:00 p.m. arrives, city ordinances against noise pollution do have mercy, and the men of the street – lawn care still proving to be a gendered activity – are forced to retire their lawn mowers and leaf blowers for the night.

Relieved, I step out again and inhale freshly cut grass, which seems to send men across the land into states of rapture, as my hearing is restored under cover of moonlight. Equilibrium and harmony return to the suburban universe until my ears perk up to another sound – this time over the resurrected serenade of a lusty cardinal.

It is a primal, almost guttural cry: "Yeee-ah!"

"Did you say something?" I ask Ronaldo, who I can see is making a mental note to mow the lawn first thing in the morning.

"Hmmm?"

"I heard a voice. More like a cry."

"Must be the cardinals," Ronaldo murmurs.

"Must be," I say, overcome by the image of white men in striped pajamas hitting a ball across a flat green lawn.

Startling Lawn Fact #6: Lawn mowers and other household yard maintenance equipment generate enough noise pollution to seriously impact wildlife, including their ability to communicate, mate, navigate and forage. But humans are also adversely affected by the cumulative noise of lawn mowers, weed whackers and, perhaps the biggest culprit of all, leaf blowers. Hearing issues such as tinnitus occur after just two hours of hearing a leaf blower fifteen metres away, and most leaf blowers in the suburbs are active just beneath one's window. A gasoline-powered lawn mower generates over one hundred decibels (electric mowers around seventy-five decibels) and hearing loss occurs around ninety decibels.[13]

Startling Lawn Facts

After thirty-five years in Canada, my siblings and I planned a reunion in Halifax, which sadly did not include our mother, who passed away in 2005, or our father, who passed away in 2019. Our family was reduced by the loss of our parents but increased by the addition of my nieces and nephew, and our spouses, each of them fellow immigrants from places like Guatemala, Egypt and India. The reunion was precipitated by the return of my brother, Reza, to Canada after many years abroad with his family. It seemed like the right moment to commemorate other kinds of histories of arrival symbolized by that old rental apartment on Cunard Street, our first home in this land.

In this last image, you will see a bit of the Commons cropped from Google Earth, still exactly as it was all those years ago: front and centre is the "gated" fountain, off to the left is one of several baseball diamonds and at the far-right corner is our Cunard Street apartment on the upper-left two floors of the quaint red Scottish dormer-style building. Looking out at the Commons, a vast green tract of land (albeit reduced in size since King George's historic bequest), I realized that thirty-five years had done little to change this view, almost as if it had been preserved for the benefit of our reunion.

Garden Inventories

But it was comforting to find the place exactly as it had been – to a naturalized citizen for whom such signposts of memory are few and far between, the sameness of it all gave me a sense of history in this land.

Halifax is fossilized as a place of beginnings and endings for us: a beginning filled with the aspirations and trepidations of all new immigrants but also the end of our time together as a family living under the same roof. The Pakistani handicraft wholesale business my father had gambled on bringing a touch of exotic elegance to Canadian homes was, like my brother's passion for cricket in a baseball-playing culture, dead on arrival. Exquisitely carved onyx and hand-etched brass was no match – at least in the Maritimes of the 1980s before HomeSense and Pier 1 Imports made global consumers of us all – for Old World porcelain like Royal Doulton teacups and royal faces gracing Royal Doulton teacups, much less for New World bric-a-brac, like wooden ducks, wall-mounted fish and, yes, even baseball paraphernalia.

The launde on which we commonly grazed as a nuclear family could no longer sustain us, and we each moved on to different pastures – my siblings and I opting for career paths that were not dependent on the fickle trends and whims of commerce and consumerism. In fact, reversals of family fortune liberated us kids to trade in our uncommonly privileged gymkhana-idling childhoods for more commonly hard-won occupations, as we sometimes plodded and sometimes ploughed our way through university, setting our sights on careers in academia (myself and Reza) or the non-profit sector (Nooreen). Despite some of their own missteps, my parents recognized and celebrated every one of these academic achievements, expressing their commonplace immigrant faith in the power of a Western education.

Startling Lawn Facts

It was a scorcher of a day, unusual for the kind of chilly Maritime summers I had experienced during my eight years in Halifax, from 1987 to 1995. My young nieces, a toddler and a five-year-old, were getting tired and overheated so we crossed the Robie and Cunard intersection to scope out a shaded place to rest on the Commons. There were some youngish trees lining the sidewalks, but on the Commons itself there was nowhere to retreat from the sun, until a small cluster of shrubs appeared like an oasis. As we sprawled across the lawn, I looked out at the not-one-but-eight baseball diamonds the Commons was designed to accommodate. At the epicentre of these lawn-diamonds sat the Commons' sole decorative feature: a circular pool with a fountain cordoned off from the public by an iron fence, as if the military folks at the old armoury were called upon to defend municipal water features from commoners like us.

Hydrated and nourished, my nieces amused themselves by scouring the ground for the one or two dandelions to have escaped decapitation by lawn mower.

And then I heard it. A voice grumbling, "What's the point of all this green space without any flowers or trees!"

Startled, I turned to look at our old apartment, convinced I'd see my mother, cup of tea in hand, standing by the big bay window.

"It's the Commons, Aunty – you know, for baseball and stuff!" my teen nephew said, rolling his eyes at me.

"Of course! How silly of me!" I winked back and propped myself up on my elbows.

With the sun shining down on us as brightly as it once had in the *lands that were*, the Commons looked less like an immaculate green carpet designed for the chosen few, and more like the gathering place for which it was once intended in this old colonial outpost.

Garden Inventories

It was hardly a perfect refuge, deficient as it was in trees and shade and an accessible water feature. And it still had a way to go in embracing Indigenous concepts of shared space and community, such as *Mawiomi*, the Mi'kmaw term for *gathering*, though the City of Halifax has since come to include a formal acknowledgement that the Commons is on ancestral and traditional Mi'kmaw lands.[14] So I had faith, because, as émigré-settlers, we too had come a long way, from indifference to a vague sense of history to awareness and appreciation of this multilayered ground beneath our feet; our compasses, once single-mindedly set to *el norte* or "True North" mythologies of the promised land, had momentarily eclipsed all other directions, but in due course we found our path to other visions and versions of this land.

As I watched my little nieces play on the grass, I was reminded of a seventeen-year-old girl sitting on a bench in downtown Halifax, which lay just a few streets beyond the clock tower at the horizon's edge on Citadel Hill. As she waited for her father to get some business permit or other, her ice-cold fingers emerged from tugged sweater sleeves to shake the hand of a stranger who'd come out of the Mi'kmaw Native Friendship Centre to greet her – and most likely to see if she was all right, shivering and alone as she was on a city bench in the middle of summer.

In our tiny pocket of shade by the shrub cluster, I felt a familiar prickle of arctic air and reached for a chilled can of lemonade. I inhaled the freshly cut grass at the Commons' perimeter, content to be in the company of this eclectic family, each of us comfortably sliding, since that first Sunday morning in our flannel pajamas, into home base.

Startling Lawn Facts

Startling Lawn Fact #7: The smell of freshly cut grass is the wounded lawn's chemical amber alert, as the freshly mown grass emits organic compounds when under attack. The next time you nostalgically inhale such a fragrance you might not want to recall this startling fact.

Not Your Garden-Variety Settlement Story

i. The Double Vision of the Twice-Displaced

We are novice tree planters and gardeners, studying with survivalist zeal the fluvial dips and alluvial turns of the Grand River watershed. We have followed different routes but our destination is, like yours, a place to put down roots. We two, from distant continents and lands, are grafted into one here, sharing, as we do, the émigré's affliction: the contrapuntal vision of the twice-displaced. An acute awareness of simultaneous dimensions. Blessed and cursed to forever see two lands, two rivers, two of everything (and sometimes even multiples). Where pomelo trees and tamarinds, ginger flower and hibiscus cast shadows on Colonial Acres, this brashly named suburban landscape, reminding us of other places. What kind of garden does one plant with the double vision of a drunkard?

ii. Weather Stories

We battled ever colder climes before we reached this Carolinian life zone. In Montreal, we gardened in the St. Lawrence Lowlands, taking ancestral cues from my partner's Mayan heritage, planting beans, corn and squash in close companionship. Little did we know this humble trinity bears its own familial name, the "Three Sisters," along the ancient highway. There must be other weather stories here, telling us of times the peoples of the south exchanged gardening tips and seeds and meals and close companionship with the peoples of the north. A time when this great hemisphere, now dismembered like a butchered turkey, was ungated, unmapped and fluid like the rivers that sustain it. If we spend more time listening to these other tales, the weather might appear less all-consuming.

iii. And Fruit Abundant

Allah hath promised to Believers gardens under which rivers flow in the eternal afterlife. Have we not arrived in such a place? Is this to be our Jannah, our Garden Paradise? For so it goes, those admitted here will dwell among trees layered with fruit abundant: date, pomegranate, lemon, fig. Such riverine commandments could be mistaken, to a child born in the mirage-laden heat of the Indian subcontinent, for a sign, celestial: All gardens must bear fruit! Apple, pear, peach, cherry, plum seem the obvious choice

Not Your Garden-Variety Settlement Story

but, as I come to learn, these pie-worthy fillers are transplants, too. Imposters, denizens, non-native, one and all. So where have all the native fruiters gone? Pawpaw, chokecherry, red mulberry, wild grape, Juneberry, staghorn sumac. Might I have seen their arching boughs on the banks of conservation creeks and the no-trespassing slopes of storm drains? Unceremoniously denied the horticulturist's stamp of approval. Tucked out of sight and out of mind in nursery clearance bins, marked down with "buyer beware" labels for their "messy" profiles and "invasive" dispositions. But who is invading whom in these postlapsarian palimpsests where non-native rivals like European buckthorns and crimson queen Japanese maples wage botanical warfare? One can only hope that hell hath no fury like a fruit tree scorned.

iv. So Much More than Fifty Shades of Green

In this *land that is*, our learning curve is steep. Far steeper than the arable hills and dandelion lawns of a watershed pastoral. Like Genghis Khan and Catharine Parr Traill, we must tie up the laces of our weather-storied sneakers and walk stealthily, alert, like double agents, both resident and alien. We must catalogue and describe, like Ibn Khaldun or Herodotus before him, everything we see, before we don the gardener's mitt or wield a pair of secateurs. We must make mental registers of our neighbours' gardens in the effort to adapt, acculturate, blend in. But the drunkard's double vision is playing tricks on us again. The contrapuntal lens of the twice-displaced has left us colour-blind and all we see is fifty shades of green, green, green in this land of evergreens borne out against a Payne's grey sky. We crave, like hungry artists, the palette of that other place with its saturated pigments. Thankfully, the story's always changing where nothing is as it first appears. Or perhaps it is the act of looking twice, looking slow, looking long, that spins the dial on the colour wheel: red oak, blue spruce, black walnut, green ash, yellow birch, silver maple, white pine. There is so much more than first appears to the migrant still nursing old wounds of rupture from *the land that was.* And like the capillary-red willow roots bursting through the banks of the Grand River, we feel our pulse, we catch our breath, we rest. At home. At last.

Acknowledgements

I am grateful to live and work in the Grand River region, traditional lands of the Haudenosaunee Confederacy of the Six Nations.

To my editor and publisher, Noelle Allen, thank you for providing the space and time to write this book with the assurance of a welcoming home at Wolsak & Wynn, a publishing house that prides itself on its deep and reciprocal relationship with this land. It's been a genuine pleasure to work on this project with you and your brilliant team, including Ashley Hisson and Jen Rawlinson.

To our neighbours: Diane Freeman, City of Waterloo Ward 4 Councillor, is owed a special thanks for taking the time to speak with me about her own research; the data she provided helped me construct a sociohistorical portrait of Colonial Acres. Rod Becker let me grill him for nuggets of insight into our neighbourhood;

his enthusiasm and knowledge are truly infectious. Claudia Knorr administers an online neighbourhood group that keeps us engaged and connected. Chris and Martina Boyer offer their support and friendship in equal measure – we are at home in your company. And all our other neighbours who share a deep appreciation for this tree-lined, garden-loving collective, and see in it something worth honouring and protecting – being part of such a community makes this project especially rewarding.

To the experts and activists: My sincere thanks to Dr. David A. Galbraith, Head of Science at the Royal Botanical Gardens of Ontario, as well as Jon L. Peter, Curator and Manager of Plant Records at the Royal Botanical Gardens of Ontario, for so kindly sharing their time and expertise. To my friend and colleague, Dr. Jing Jing Chang, for gifting me the name of the rose in Mandarin. To co-founder of the Waterloo Book Fair Caroline Topperman, for reading one of the early chapters, and for championing local authors of the region. To Dr. Deborah Bowen, for permission to reproduce my prose-poem "Not Your Garden-Variety Settlement Story," originally written for the forthcoming anthology *Poetry in Place*.

To both my siblings, Reza Pirbhai and Nooreen Pirbhai, for letting me dip my toe into our family's ocean of story.

This book is clearly written in conversation with Ronaldo, fellow émigré, fellow gardener, fellow teacher, fellow nature enthusiast and walking companion – thank you for always holding my hand in this land and in all the other lands we might travel and find home in together.

Notes

The Land That Is

1   See Lorraine Johnson, ed., *The Natural Treasures of Carolinian Canada: Discovering the Rich Natural Diversity of Ontario's Southwestern Heartland* (Toronto: Lorimer, 2007).

2   As Dr. Amy Cardinal Christianson explains, "cultural burning" typically involves "low-intensity, small-scale burns that are community driven and practiced by Indigenous fire-keepers around the world." See "Canada Needs Indigenous-Led Fire Stewardship, New Research Finds," *UBC News*, April 26, 2022, https://news.ubc.ca/2022/04/26/canada-needs-indigenous-led-fire-stewardship/.

3   See E. Reginald Good, "Colonizing a People: Mennonite Settlement in Waterloo Township," in *Earth, Water, Air and Fire: Studies in Canadian Ethnohistory*, ed. David T. McNab (Waterloo: Wilfrid Laurier University Press, 1999), 152–88, for a historical overview of settlement patterns in the Waterloo township. (Good refers to the fact that until the conquest of New France in 1759–60, the British recognized southern Ontario as the territory

of the Ojibwe, or the Mississaugas, as they came to be known on the northern shores of Lake Ontario.)

4   In his introductory chapter, historian and Royal Society of Canada fellow David T. McNab defines "'treaty' . . . as the 'treating of matters with a view to settlement; discussion of terms, conference, negotiation.' The treaty-making process in the Aboriginal context is the series of conferences held, under the Covenant Chain of Silver, which has continued to be the fundamental relationship or framework between Aboriginal and non-Aboriginal people, and which metaphorically binds or covenants them together." David T. McNab, *Circles of Time: Aboriginal Land Rights and Resistance in Ontario* (Waterloo: Wilfrid Laurier University Press, 1999), 8.

5   Of course, there are innumerable historical accounts of Partition, but personal narratives about Partition from the diaspora's perspective, especially the South Asian Canadian diaspora, are few and far between. I would recommend Madhur Anand's *This Red Line Goes Straight to Your Heart* (Toronto: Strange Light, 2020), an experimental memoir that captures the way Partition history was a traumatic lived experience for many South Asians who eventually settled in Canada, and a familial legacy for subsequent generations.

6   "Residential Neighbourhoods," in *Cultural Heritage Landscape Inventory 2019* (Waterloo: City of Waterloo, 2019), https://www.waterloo.ca/en/government/resources/Documents/Cityadministration/Cultural-Heritage-Landscapes-Study/2-Residential-Neighbourhoods.pdf. See also the City of Waterloo Museum's "The Birth of Waterloo's Suburban Neighbourhoods" presentation: https://www.waterloo.ca/en/museum/presentations.aspx#The-Birth-of-Waterloos-Suburban-Neighbourhoods.

7   As E. Reginald Good attests, "Mennonite settlement patterns followed Indian settlement patterns" along Indigenous trails, those "original avenues" across the Niagara Escarpment and deep into the Grand River valley ("Colonizing a People," 164–65).

8   General references of this nature to the history of the Colonial Acres neighbourhood are largely culled from Elizabeth Bloomfield, *Waterloo Township through Two Centuries* (Kitchener, ON: Waterloo Historical

Notes

Society, 1995). Also, from data provided by Waterloo Ward 4 councillor Diane Freeman in March 2022, based on research complied, with the assistance of interested neighbours living in the Colonial Acres neighbourhood, and in consultation with the Kitchener Public Library archivist in 2017. As Freeman notes, this research helped to inform the creation of Waterloo's first Heritage Landscape District.

9   Bloomfield, *Waterloo Township through Two Centuries*, 27.

10   I am grateful to Rod Becker for taking the time to share these stories of our neighbourhood with me, and for his knowledge of the area.

11   A local Mennonite family provides a tour of their sugar maple farm as an example of farming practices in the greater St. Jacobs Mennonite community. I was struck by how a deciduous forest once teeming with native trees such as the black walnut and red oak had been felled to make room for the sugar maple, which now functions as a monocrop plantation. See the Maple Sugar Bush Tour (currently on hiatus) operated by the St. Jacobs Horse Drawn Tours: https://stjacobshorsedrawntours.com/mapleSugarBushTours.html.

12   "About," Six Nations of the Grand River, https://www.sixnations.ca/about.

Contrapuntal Gardeners

1   Edward Said, "The Mind of Winter: Reflections on Life in Exile," *Harper's Magazine*, September 1984, 49–55.

2   Sikandra is the name of a walled garden surrounding Akbar's tomb, which the emperor commissioned during his lifetime. It is situated in Agra, the former seat of Mughal power, now a city in the Indian state of Uttar Pradesh. See also Jacob Dickie, "The Mughal Garden: Gateway to Paradise," *Muqarnas: An Annual on Islamic Art and Architecture* 3 (June 1985): 133.

3   Martin's Family Fruit Farm claims to have been farming for over two centuries, growing from a farm of "a hundred trees in 1971 to more than half a million trees on over 700 acres today" located on Lobsinger

Line, less than a mile, in either direction, from St. Jacobs Farmers' Market and the town of St. Jacobs. "Our Story," Martin's Family Fruit Farm, https://martinsapples.com/.

4 Edwinna von Baeyer, "McIntosh Apple," *The Canadian Encyclopedia*, September 30, 2019, https://www.thecanadianencyclopedia.ca/en/article/mcintosh-apple.

5 *Cambridge Learner's Dictionary*, s.v. "bear fruit," https://dictionary.cambridge.org/dictionary/learner-english/bear-fruit.

6 Christine Ammer, *The American Heritage Dictionary of Idioms*, 2nd ed. (Boston: Houghton Mifflin Harcourt, 2013), 32.

7 Samuel Strickland, quoted in Carol Martin, *A History of Canadian Gardening* (Toronto: McArthur, 2000), 49.

8 Martin, *A History of Canadian Gardening*, 68.

9 Holy Quran, Surah al Waqi'ah, 9:72. Translations can be found online: https://quran.com/9/72?translations=17,18,19,20,22,84,85,21,95,101.

10 Holy Quran, Surah al Waqi'ah, 56:27–33, https://quran.com/56/27-33.

11 This illustration titled the *Bagh-e-Wafa*, or *Garden of Fidelity*, is found in Emperor Babur's multivolume illustrated memoir, the *Baburnama*, and depicts Babur's first garden, which is said to have contained oranges, lemons and pomegranates. There are numerous editions of the *Baburnama*, but for an illustrated edition see Som Prakash Verma, *The Illustrated Baburnama* (Abingdon, UK: Routledge India, 2016). The image reproduced here is sourced from Verma's text: Plate 42, page 134. As per this text, the original is housed at the New Delhi Museum: Folio 121a.

12 Sadaf Fatma, "Gardens in Mughal Gujarat," *Proceedings of the Indian History Congress* 72 (2011): 441–52, http://www.jstor.org/stable/44146737.

13 Fatma, "Gardens in Mughal Gujarat," 442.

14 Dr. Reza Pirbhai, email to author, July 11, 2020.

15 "Pakistan mulberry," One Green World, https://onegreenworld.com/product/pakistan-mulberry/.

Notes

16   See Widget Finn, "The Turbulent History of the Mulberry," *Telegraph*, September 10, 2015. As Paul E. Hatcher and Nick Battey sum up this doomed enterprise, "the attempts at sericulture in England and North America were dogged by failures in plant identification, botanical prejudices and unfounded assumptions stemming from a lack of scientific investigation in the area." See Chapter 5 ("Silkworms and Mulberries") in Paul Hatcher and Nick Battey, *Biological Diversity: Exploiters and Exploited* (Chichester, UK: Wiley-Blackwell, 2011). EBook.

17   Jon L. Peter, email to author, June 29, 2020.

18   Dr. David Galbraith, email to author, June 24, 2020.

19   As noted in the North Carolina Extension Gardener Toolbox, "many gardeners feel [these trees] have no place in the home landscape as a fruit or specimen tree" for they are at once "messy," "weedy," "poisonous to humans" and a "problem for children." *"Morus alba,"* North Carolina Extension Gardener Plant Toolbox, https://plants.ces.ncsu.edu/plants/morus-alba/.

20   "Mulberry," DeGroot's Nurseries, August 3, 2019, https://degroots.ca/mulberry/.

21   Shakespeare's story of Pyramus and Thisbe appears in the comedy *A Midsummer Night's Dream* and is adapted from Ovid's *Metamorphoses*, Book IV, where two lovers defy their families' interdictions, arranging to meet in secret under a mulberry tree. (Likely also the basis of inspiration for *Romeo and Juliet*.)

22   William Shakespeare, *A Midsummer Night's Dream*, Act 5, Scene 1, lines 152–53, Folger Shakespeare Library, https://www.folger.edu/explore/shakespeares-works/a-midsummer-nights-dream/read/5/1/.

23   William Shakespeare, *Coriolanus*, Act 3, Scene 2, lines 98–99, Folger Shakespeare Library, https://www.folger.edu/explore/shakespeares-works/coriolanus/read/3/2/.

By Any Other Name

1   Jamaica Kincaid, "Flowers of Evil," *New Yorker*, October 1992, 158.

2   Majid Sheikh, "Harking Back: Mystery of the Rajput Empress Mariam Zamani," *Dawn*, March 22, 2020, https://www.dawn.com/news/1542722.

3   Thanks to my brother, Dr. Reza Pirbhai, for this insight. Though I can tap his intellectual resources directly, via phone calls and WhatsApp exchanges, I also refer you to his biographical work, *Fatima Jinnah: Mother of the Nation* (Cambridge: Cambridge University Press, 2017), which includes a brief explanation of this ethnography.

4   References are sourced from Catharine Parr Traill, *Canadian Wild Flowers* (Almonte, ON: Algrove Publishing, 2003), originally published in 1868 in Montreal by J. Lovell. The recent edition also includes the original book's gorgeous botanical illustrations by Agnes Fitzgibbon. See also Carol Martin, *A History of Canadian Gardening* (Toronto: McArthur, 2000).

5   As is noted on the home page of its website, "The *International Code of Nomenclature for algae, fungi, and plants* is the set of rules and recommendations that govern the scientific naming of all organisms traditionally treated as algae, fungi, or plants, whether fossil or non-fossil, including blue-green algae (*Cyanobacteria*), chytrids, oomycetes, slime moulds, and photosynthetic protists with their taxonomically related non-photosynthetic groups (but excluding Microsporidia). Before 2011 it was called the *International Code of Botanical Nomenclature* (ICBN)." *International Code of Nomenclature for algae, fungi, and plants*, International Association for Plant Taxonomy, https://www.iapt-taxon.org/nomen/main.php.

6   Allen Paterson, *The History of the Rose* (London: Collins, 1983). It should be noted that the rose's botanical names and genealogy outlined in this section are drawn from Paterson's work.

7   Paterson, *History of the Rose*, 44.

8   Hafez (or Hafiz), "Ghazal 128," in *The Poems of Hafez*, trans. Reza Ordoubadian (Bethesda, MD: Ibex, 2006), n.p.

Notes

9   Mirza Ghalib, "Untitled," in *Ghalib: Interpretations: Translations of Selected Verse*, trans. Riza Ahmed (Karachi, Pakistan: Ferozsons, 1996), 28.

10   Abdur Razzaq (referred to as Abdur Razzak on the Indian Rose Federation "About Us" page) was a Persian historian and traveller chosen as ambassador to India by Shah Rukh of Persia in the fifteenth century; he chronicled his travels to India in his book, *Matla-al-Sa'dayn*. This quote is taken from "About Us," Indian Rose Federation, https://www.indianrosefederation.com/aboutus.html.

11   Daniel Coleman, *Yardwork: A Biography of an Urban Place* (Hamilton, ON: James Street North Books, 2017), 23.

12   Jonathan Shaughnessy, "The 'World' of Contemporary Gallery B104," *National Gallery of Canada Magazine*, December 14, 2016, https://www.gallery.ca/magazine/exhibitions/the-world-of-contemporary-gallery-b104.

13   I encourage you to view Christi Belcourt's *Water Song* (2010–11), housed at the National Gallery of Canada.

Anthropology of the Cottage, or a (Second?) Slice of Precambrian Pie

1   Adam Carter, "Ontario Premier Doug Ford Briefly Visited Cottage After Asking Residents Not To," *CBC News*, May 8, 2020, https://www.cbc.ca/news/canada/toronto/ford-cottage-covid-19-coronavirus-1.5561167.

2   Daniel Coleman, *Yardwork: A Biography of an Urban Place* (Hamilton, ON: James Street North Books, 2017), 29.

3   Coleman, *Yardwork*, 29.

4   Julia Harrison, *A Timeless Place: The Ontario Cottage* (Vancouver: UBC Press, 2013), 2.

5   Elamin Abdelmahmoud, "Breaking the Colour Code of the Canadian Cottage Experience," *Cottage Life*, March 20, 2019, accessed October 10, 2021, https://cottagelife.com/general/breaking-the-colour-code-of-the-canadian-cottage-experience/.

Garden Inventories

6   For Drew Hayden Taylor, cottage country is an extension of the Indigenous-settler encounter. His play *Cottagers and Indians*, first performed at Toronto's Tarragon Theatre in 2018, epitomizes the conflictual nature of that encounter. The play is available in a published edition: *Cottagers and Indians* (Vancouver: Talonbooks, 2019).

7   Peter A. Stevens, "A Little Place in the (Next) Country: Negotiating Nature and Nation in 1970s Ontario," *Journal of Canadian Studies* 47, no. 3 (Fall 2013): 42–66.

8   Kelly Grant, "Let Us Back into Our Cottages," *Globe and Mail*, August 16, 2008, https://www.theglobeandmail.com/news/national/let-us-back-into-our-cottages/article658498/.

9   See Jonathan Bordo, "Jack Pine – Wilderness Sublime or the Erasure of the Aboriginal Presence from the Landscape," *Journal of Canadian Studies* 27, no. 4 (Winter 1992–93): 98–128. See also Andrew Baldwin, Laura Cameron and Audrey Kobayashi, eds., *Rethinking the Great White North: Race, Nature, and the Historical Geographies of Whiteness in Canada* (Vancouver: UBC Press, 2011).

10   Patricia Jasen, *Wild Things: Nature, Culture, and Tourism in Ontario, 1790–1914* (Toronto: University of Toronto Press, 1995).

11   Peter A. Stevens, "Decolonizing Cottage Country," *Active History*, February 22, 2018, http://activehistory.ca/2018/02/decolonizing-cottage-country/.

12   Stevens, "Decolonizing Cottage Country."

13   *Britannica*, s.v. "Space Invaders," last modified October 6, 2023, https://www.britannica.com/topic/Space-Invaders. (*Space Invaders* was created by Tomohiro Nishikado, in 1978.)

Garden Inventories

1   This definition was culled and paraphrased from a variety of government and non-profit organizations working for the protection of native

Notes

species in North America, including the Government of Ontario, "Invasive Species in Ontario," June 11, 2019, updated May 4, 2023, https://www.ontario.ca/page/invasive-species-ontario; Conservation Ontario, "Invasive Species," https://conservationontario.ca/conservation-authorities/watershed-stewardship/invasive-species; the Canadian Council on Native Species, "Invasive Species," https://canadainvasives.ca/invasive-species/; the Ontario Invasive Plant Council, "Species," https://www.ontarioinvasiveplants.ca/invasive-plants/species/; and U.S. Forest Reserve, "Native Plant Materials," https://www.fs.usda.gov/wildflowers/Native_Plant_Materials/whatare.shtml.

2   Catharine Parr Traill, *Canadian Wild Flowers* (Montreal: J. Lovell, 1868; Almonte, ON: Algrove Publishing, 2003), 14.

3   Robin Wall Kimmerer, *Braiding Sweetgrass: Indigenous Wisdom, Scientific Knowledge, and the Teachings of Plants* (Minneapolis: Milkweed Editions, 2013), 208.

4   Please refer to sources listed under note #1 above.

5   Hayley Anderson, *Invasive Common (European) Buckthorn* (Rhamnus cathartica): *Best Management Practices in Ontario* (Peterborough: Ontario Invasive Plant Council, 2021), https://www.ontarioinvasiveplants.ca/wp-content/uploads/2016/06/OIPC_BMP_Buckthorn.pdf.

6   See *The Natural Treasures of Carolinian Canada*, ed. Lorraine Johnson (Toronto: Carolinian Canada Coalition, 2007).

7   City of Waterloo, By-Law No. 08-026, *A By-Law Respecting the Conservation of Trees in Woodlands*, June 18, 2008, https://www.regionofwaterloo.ca/en/resources/Bylaws/By-law-08-026.PDF.

8   Thomas King, "A Coyote Columbus Story," in *One Good Story, That One: Stories* (Toronto: HarperCollins, 1993), 119–28.

9   Kimmerer, *Braiding Sweetgrass*, 214. Kimmerer speaks of both human and non-human forms of "naturalization" to a place, such that anything foreign or non-native to a place should ideally live in a reciprocal relationship with the land, and "to take care of this land as if our lives and the lives of all our relatives depend on it" (214–15).

10   Harini Nagendra and Seema Mundoli, "Babur to WWII to Sonia Gandhi, all Connected through the Tamarind Tree in India," ThePrint, June 9, 2019, https://theprint.in/pageturner/excerpt/babur-to-wwii-to-sonia-gandhi-all-connected-through-the-tamarind-tree-in-india/247670/.

11   Nagendra and Mundoli, "Babur to WWII to Sonia Gandhi."

12   N.C. Shah, "Tamarindus indica – Introduction in India and Culinary, Medicinal and Industrial Uses," *Asian Agri-History* 18, no. 4 (2014): 343–55.

13   Ken Fern, "*Tamarindus indica*," Useful Tropical Plants Database, https://tropical.theferns.info/viewtropical.php?id=Tamarindus+indica.

14   Kimmerer, *Braiding Sweetgrass*, 213.

15   Jean "Binta" Breeze, quoted in Elizabeth M. DeLoughrey, Renée K. Gosson and George B. Handley, introduction to *Caribbean Literature and the Environment: Between Nature and Culture*, ed. DeLoughrey, Gosson and Handley (Charlottesville: University of Virginia Press, 2005), 12.

16   Kimmerer, *Braiding Sweetgrass*, 46–47.

17   *Pawpaw* and *papaya* are used interchangeably in tropical cultures. This may be because the pawpaw native to the Carolinian life zone was likely renamed as such by European explorers because it reminded them of the tropical papaya. See also Mari-Len De Guzman, "Indigenous Tree Bears Rich History, Culture for Western," *Western News*, September 30, 2021, https://news.westernu.ca/2021/09/indigenous-pawpaw-trees-at-western/.

Startling Lawn Facts

1   *New World Encyclopedia*, s.v. "Grass," https://www.newworldencyclopedia.org/entry/Grass.

2   The italicized segments in this chapter provide information paraphrased or synthesized from a variety of sources. The two major monographs on the subject are Virginia Scott Jenkins, *The Lawn: A History of an American Obsession* (Washington, DC: Smithsonian Books, 1994) and Ted Steinberg,

Notes

American Green: The Obsessive Quest for the Perfect Lawn (New York: W.W. Norton, 2006). Other articles consulted include those directly cited in this chapter as well as Christopher Borrelli, "How About Rethinking a Cultural Icon? The Front Lawn," *Chicago Tribune*, October 7, 2017, https://www.chicagotribune.com/entertainment/ct-ent-lawns-20171002-story.html, and Elizabeth Kolbert, "Turf War," *New Yorker*, July 14, 2008, https://www.newyorker.com/magazine/2008/07/21/turf-war-elizabeth-kolbert.

3 Rory Dusoir, "The History of Lawns," *Gardens Illustrated*, July 4, 2022, https://www.gardensillustrated.com/feature/the-history-of-lawns/.

4 Middle English Compendium, s.v. "laund(e," https://quod.lib.umich.edu/m/middle-english-dictionary/dictionary/MED24859.

5 "Halifax Common," Halifax Military Heritage Preservation Society, https://hmhps.ca/sites/halifax-common.

6 Megan Garber, "The Life and Death of the American Lawn," *The Atlantic*, August 28, 2015, https://www.theatlantic.com/entertainment/archive/2015/08/the-american-lawn-a-eulogy/402745/.

7 Quoted in Saleah Blancaflor, "120 Years After Philippine Independence from Spain, Hispanic Influence Remains," *NBC News*, October 1, 2018, https://www.nbcnews.com/news/asian-america/120-years-after-philippine-independence-spain-hispanic-influence-remains-n912916.

8 Quoted in Borrelli, "How About Rethinking a Cultural Icon?"

9 *The Nature of Things*, season 59, episode 2, "Grasslands: A Hidden Wilderness," directed by Alex Burr, featuring David Suzuki, aired September 27, 2019, on CBC, https://www.cbc.ca/natureofthings/episodes/grasslands-a-hidden-wilderness.

10 Jenkins, *The Lawn*, 18–19.

11 Ferris Jabr, "Outgrowing the Traditional Grass Lawn," *Scientific American*, July 29, 2013, https://blogs.scientificamerican.com/brainwaves/outgrowing-the-traditional-grass-lawn/.

12 See Krystal D'Costa, "The American Obsession with Lawns," *Scientific American*, May 3, 2017, https://blogs.scientificamerican.com/anthropology-in-practice/the-american-obsession-with-lawns/.

Garden Inventories

13 See Joel M. Lerner, "Not All Gardening Tools Are Created Equal," *Washington Post*, March 25, 2011, https://www.washingtonpost.com/realestate/not-all-gardening-tools-are-created-equal/2011/03/17/AF7yerWB_story.html; see also Jason Osler, "More Municipalities Blowing Off Noisy Gardening Tools," *CBC News*, June 7, 2018, https://www.cbc.ca/news/canada/more-municipalities-blowing-off-noisy-landscaping-tools-1.4695956; see also "4 Ways that Noise Pollution Can Impact Wildlife (and 4 Ways to Help)," Wildlife Habitat Council, April 15, 2021, https://www.wildlifehc.org/4-ways-that-noise-pollution-can-impact-wildlife-and-4-ways-to-help/.

14 Mi'kmaq Nation, "Mawiomi," http://micmac-nsn.gov/mawiomi.

Mariam Pirbhai is the author of a debut novel titled *Isolated Incident* (Mawenzi House, 2022) and a short story collection titled *Outside People and Other Stories* (Inanna Publications, 2017), winner of the IPPY Gold Medal for Multicultural Fiction and the American BookFest Award for the Short Story. Pirbhai is a professor of English at Wilfrid Laurier University, where she teaches and specializes in postcolonial studies and creative writing. She is also the author or editor of several academic books on the global South Asian diaspora, including *Mythologies of Migration, Vocabularies of Indenture: Novels of the South Asian Diaspora in Africa, the Caribbean, and Asia-Pacific* (University of Toronto Press, 2009) and *Critical Perspectives on Indo-Caribbean Women's Literature* (Routledge, 2013). Pirbhai has served as president of CAPS (Canadian Association for Postcolonial Studies, formerly CACLALS), Canada's longest running scholarly association devoted to postcolonial and global anglophone literatures. Pirbhai is the daughter of Pakistani immigrants whose arrival in Canada followed a circuitous route from England, the United Arab Emirates and the Philippines. She and her husband live in Waterloo, Ontario.